CLAIMS AND CLUES-

THE ART OF INSURANCE INVESTIGATION

CHENNAMALLIKARJUN C BHUSANUR

Made with ♥ on the Notion Press Platform
www.notionpress.com

"To the memory of my beloved younger brother, the Late Vijayakumar Bhusanur. Forever in my heart."

And to

The Unsung Heroes: Insurance Investigators. Insurance investigators are the unsung guardians of the insurance industry.

Often working behind the scenes, they play a critical role in maintaining the integrity of the system. These individuals, primarily self-taught and resourcefully independent, dedicate their careers to unraveling complex cases with minimal recognition or reward.

Their work is essential in combating fraud, accurately assessing claims, and protecting the interests of both insurers and policyholders. Despite the challenges and pressures of their role, insurance investigators persevere, driven by a commitment to fairness and justice.

Contents

Contents

Contents

Contents

Message From Insurance Sector Leader

Thank you, Bhusanur ji, for authoring such a wonderful and insightful book on real-life experiences in insurance claims investigation. Your dedication in documenting these cases and transforming your field knowledge into an engaging narrative is truly commendable.

The book offers a rich blend of practical wisdom and professional insights, making it an invaluable resource for investigators, claims professionals, and anyone interested in understanding the nuances of insurance fraud and its investigation process.

Your sincere efforts in sharing these experiences will undoubtedly inspire and guide many in the industry. My heartfelt appreciation and best wishes to you for taking the time to record and share such important and eventful investigation stories with the wider audience.

Once again, thank you for this remarkable contribution to the insurance fraternity.

Warm regards,

Dr. Sajiv Dwivedi
President & Head – Investigation & Loss Mitigation
BAJAJ ALLIANZ GENERAL INSURANCE

Enter Caption

Preface

The insurance investigator's world was an entanglement of paperwork, phone calls, and endless claims. A monotonous routine punctuated by the occasional bizarre case. Most days were spent poring over documents, searching for inconsistencies, red flags, or simply the mundane truth. Car accidents, house fires, and medical claims were the bread and butter, each a puzzle with its own unique set of pieces.

There was a certain satisfaction in piecing together a claim, in determining the legitimacy of a loss. But more often than not, the work was a grind, a necessary evil in the world of insurance. Yet, it was precisely this monotony that sharpened the investigator's mind. The ability to spot the unusual within the ordinary was a skill honed over years of examining the mundane.

A new claim landed on the desk. A blast accident at the site of construction, seemingly straightforward. A death of an employee, and a standard insurance policy. But as the investigator delved deeper, a nagging sense of doubt crept in. Something about the accident report felt off, a dissonance in the symphony of facts.

Acknowledgements

I would like to express my sincere gratitude to my wife, Nirmala, for her unwavering encouragement and support throughout this endeavor. Her belief in me has been a constant source of motivation.

I am also deeply indebted to my son, Akhil, for his invaluable support. His enthusiasm and willingness to help have been instrumental in the completion of this project.

Furthermore, I would like to acknowledge the invaluable assistance provided by AI platforms. These tools have been instrumental in gathering information, proofreading, and ensuring the accuracy of this work. Their capabilities have significantly enhanced the efficiency and quality of my research.

Prologue

A Stone's Throw from Truth

My career as an insurance investigator began with a bang, or rather, a thud. It was the late 1980s, and I was a novice, freshly empaneled with United India Insurance Co. Ltd., Hubballi Division. My first major case involved a tragic accident on the Konkan Railway project. A young engineer had met a grisly end, allegedly struck by a stray rock during a blast. The case was handed to me, and I was expected to determine if it was a legitimate workman's compensation claim.

At first glance, it seemed straightforward. Police reports, medical records, and witness statements painted a picture of a fatal accident. However, a niggling doubt gnawed at me. Something about the case just didn't sit right. With the skepticism of a rookie and the tenacity of a bloodhound, I dug deeper.

I consulted with physicists at Karnataka University, Dharwad. Their calculations were damning. The rock couldn't have traveled the distance required to inflict such fatal injuries. The accident theory crumbled. After duly alerting the Police on the findings the case was now a murder investigation.

The serene Konkan landscape transformed into a crime scene. I delved into the victim's personal life. It was a classic case of a love triangle gone horribly wrong. A jealous brother, a fatal attraction, and a carefully planned murder. The killer had used the blast as a perfect alibi.

The inconsistencies in the case were brought to the notice of the jurisdictional Police Head. The Police revisited the case. Justice prevailed, and the murderer was brought to book. It was a career-defining case. The satisfaction of unraveling a complex mystery and bringing a criminal to justice was intoxicating. Little did I know, this was just the beginning of a career filled with unexpected twists and turns.

A twist of fate: When appearances deceive.

Fast forward a few years. I was assigned another case, this time a third-party liability claim. A woman claimed to be permanently disabled after an accident, unable to walk without crutches. The medical reports were grim, and the case seemed cut and dried. But my earlier experience had made me cautious.

I visited the claimant's home. While waiting for her to grant us entry, I noticed something peculiar: she seemed to move with surprising ease. Curiosity piqued, I initiated surveillance. The woman was caught on camera walking without crutches, going about her daily routine as if nothing was wrong.

Further investigation revealed she was employed and had faked the entire disability to claim compensation. It was a blatant fraud. The case was a stark reminder that not every claim is genuine. It required meticulous investigation and a keen eye for detail to uncover the truth.

A Masterful Deception: Exposing the Truth Behind the Claim

The case of Mr. Gururaj's car accident was a puzzle wrapped in an enigma, smothered in a thick layer of deception. On the face of it, it was a straightforward claim of a car damaged in a collision with a mysterious tractor-trailer. However, as the investigation deepened, a web of inconsistencies and contradictions began to unravel.

The first red flag was the glaring gap in the car's insurance coverage. A period of three and a half years without insurance for a vehicle is not a mere oversight; it's a deliberate act. This, coupled with the fact that the accident occurred during a strict lockdown when traffic was minimal, raised serious doubts about the authenticity of the claim.

The medical evidence was equally perplexing. The insured claimed injuries requiring treatment at two different hospitals, yet there was no concrete medical record to substantiate these claims. The hospitals presented conflicting accounts, and the insured's attempts to influence medical professionals were evident. It was as if a carefully orchestrated play was unfolding, with the insured as the director and the rest of us as unwitting actors.

The workshop involved in repairing the car added another layer of intrigue. The haste in processing the claim, coupled with the discrepancies in the timeline, suggested a collusion between the insured and the workshop. It was as if they were in cahoots to defraud the insurance company.

As the investigation progressed, it became increasingly clear that the accident was a staged event, a carefully planned fraud. The insured's elaborate story, complete with a missing third-party vehicle and convenient medical records, began to crumble under the weight of evidence. The absence of a police complaint, the inconsistencies in the timeline, and the suspicious nature of the medical certificates painted a damning picture of a fraudulent claim.

The case was a stark reminder of the lengths people will go to for personal gain. It was a battle between truth and deception, where every piece of evidence was a clue leading us closer to the heart of the fraud. In the end, the web of lies was exposed, and the truth prevailed. It was a victory for diligent investigation and a testament to the importance of thorough scrutiny in the insurance industry.

These cases were a defining moment in my career, a baptism by fire that shaped my approach to investigations. It taught me the importance of skepticism, the power of meticulous analysis, and the unwavering pursuit of truth.

These three cases, poles apart in their nature, shaped mine as well as our Team's career as an investigators. They taught me the importance of skepticism, the power of interdisciplinary collaboration, and the unwavering pursuit of truth.

It was a journey filled with challenges, triumphs, and the occasional absurdity. But through it all, I learned that behind every claim, there's a story. And sometimes, that story is far more intriguing than you'd ever imagine.

Auto Insurance Fraud

Buckle up for a thrilling ride through the world of auto insurance fraud. Unmask the tactics used by fraudsters to exploit the auto insurance system.

CHAPTER ONE

The Elusive Threat: - A broad overview of the insurance fraud landscape in India.

The Indian insurance industry, like its global counterparts, is haunted by the specter of fraud. Unlike impulsive crimes driven by immediate gratification, insurance fraud is often a meticulously orchestrated dance of deception, performed by intelligent, organized criminals. Their motive is clear: financial gain. However, their methods are marked by a subtlety and cunning that makes detection a complex and elusive endeavor.

Recent reports have uncovered alarming trends in insurance fraud in India. According to the Times of India, fraudulent claims make up approximately 15% of all insurance claims, amounting to around 900 crores annually. Similarly, a survey by Deloitte India estimates that insurers lose close to 10% of their overall premium collections, translating to USD 6 billion annually, due to fraudulent activities.

Understanding the Perpetrators

These fraudsters are not mere opportunists; they often possess an intimate understanding of the insurance ecosystem. Their knowledge of claims procedures, risk mitigation strategies, and industry loopholes is often on par with that of seasoned insurance professionals. This deep-rooted familiarity allows them to devise sophisticated schemes that are difficult to identify and even harder to prosecute.

For instance, consider the case of a fraudulent health insurance claim where the perpetrator, a former insurance agent, used his insider knowledge to fabricate medical records and submit false claims. His understanding of the claims process enabled him to exploit procedural gaps, resulting in significant financial losses for the insurer.

Modus Operandi

The modus operandi of these criminals is characterized by meticulous planning and execution. They study insurance products and the vulnerabilities inherent in the claims process. Their operations are shrouded in secrecy, and they are adept at manipulating individuals to become unwitting accomplices. Consequently, pinpointing the exact nature of the loss and the perpetrators involved becomes a formidable challenge.

A real-world example is the infamous "Cash for Crash" scam, where fraudsters deliberately stage car accidents to claim insurance money. These staged accidents are carefully orchestrated, with fake witnesses and fabricated evidence, making it extremely challenging for insurers to detect the fraud.

Detection and Prevention

Despite the intricate nature of insurance fraud, it is not an insurmountable problem. The cornerstone of effective fraud prevention lies in the vigilance of insurance practitioners. By meticulously scrutinizing routine transactions, they can often detect anomalies that may indicate fraudulent activity.

Identifying suspicious claims is the first critical step in the fraud detection process. Statistical analysis can be a valuable tool in flagging claims that deviate from established patterns. For example, if an unusually high number of claims are submitted from a particular geographic area, it may warrant further investigation. Additionally, the insights of claims adjusters and insurance agents, who are often the first line of defense, can be instrumental in recognizing potential fraud.

Investigative Measures

To counter the multifaceted nature of insurance fraud, insurers have adopted a combination of preventive and investigative measures. Rigorous cross-verification of documents is essential to uncover inconsistencies and discrepancies. However, the fast-paced claims environment often necessitates quick decision-making, making this task challenging.

Investigations into insurance fraud can be broadly categorized as constructive or reconstructive. Constructive investigations are covert operations designed to gather evidence discreetly. For example, an investigator might pose as a customer to gather information on a suspected fraudulent claim. On the other hand, reconstructive investigations are overt inquiries conducted openly to deter potential fraudsters. This might involve interviewing witnesses and collecting physical evidence to build a case.

Role of Professional Investigators

Given the complexity of insurance fraud cases, employing professional investigators with specialized skills and resources is often imperative. These investigators must possess a deep understanding of both covert and overt investigative techniques to effectively combat the multifaceted nature of these crimes. Moreover, they must be able to work efficiently within tight timelines to minimize losses.

For instance, in a case involving a fraudulent life insurance claim, investigators might need to verify the authenticity of death certificates and interview family members to uncover the truth. Their ability to navigate sensitive situations and gather credible evidence is crucial to the success of the investigation.

Documentation and Prosecution

To ensure the successful prosecution of insurance fraud cases, meticulous documentation is essential. Investigation reports must be clear, concise, and compelling, presenting the evidence in a manner that is easily understandable to legal and judicial authorities. This documentation serves as the foundation for legal proceedings and helps ensure that justice is served.

Conclusion

In conclusion, insurance fraud in India is a sophisticated challenge that demands a comprehensive and multifaceted response. By combining vigilance, advanced analytical tools, and specialized investigative capabilities, the insurance industry can significantly reduce its vulnerability to these criminal activities. Ultimately, the success of fraud prevention efforts depends on a collaborative approach involving insurers, investigators, and law enforcement agencies. By sharing knowledge and resources, these stakeholders can create a robust defense against the elusive threat of insurance fraud, safeguarding the integrity of the insurance industry and protecting the interests of honest policyholders.

CHAPTER TWO

Common Types of Insurance Fraud – Categorizing types of insurance fraud prevalent in India.

Insurance fraud, a pervasive issue globally, has its unique characteristics in India. A complex interplay of socio-economic factors, regulatory environment, and evolving criminal tactics contributes to the diverse landscape of insurance fraud in the country.

1. Inflated Claims

This is perhaps the most common type of insurance fraud in India. Policyholders often exaggerate the extent of damage or loss to claim a higher amount than what is rightfully due. This can occur in various insurance lines, such as:

- **Motor Insurance**: Exaggerating the cost of repairs, claiming non-existent damages, or inflating the value of stolen vehicles. For example, a policyholder might claim that their car sustained severe damage in an accident when, in reality, the damage was minor.
- **Property Insurance**: Inflating the value of lost or damaged property, or fabricating losses altogether. An example could be a homeowner claiming that expensive electronics were stolen during a break-in, even though these items never existed.
- **Health Insurance**: Claiming treatments or procedures that were not undergone or exaggerating medical expenses. For instance, a policyholder might submit bills for medical procedures that were never performed.

2. Fake Claims

In this type of fraud, a claim is made for a loss that never occurred. It can involve:

- **Motor Insurance**: Staging accidents or thefts. For example, a policyholder might stage a car accident with the help of accomplices to claim insurance money.
- **Property Insurance**: Filing false claims for theft, fire, or other perils. An example could be a business owner claiming that a fire destroyed their inventory, when in fact, no such fire occurred.
- **Health Insurance**: Claiming hospitalization for a non-existent illness. For instance, a policyholder might submit a claim for a hospital stay that never happened.

3. Ghost Claims

These are claims made for a policyholder who is either deceased or non-existent. Often, these involve collusion between policyholders, beneficiaries, and unscrupulous agents or brokers. For example, an agent might continue to submit claims on behalf of a deceased policyholder, splitting the proceeds with the beneficiaries.

4. Policy Fraud

This type of fraud involves misrepresentation or concealment of material facts during the policy application process. It can include:

- **Underreporting of Risks**: Downplaying the risk profile to secure lower premiums. For example, a business might underreport the hazardous materials stored on-site to reduce insurance costs.
- **Overstating Coverage Needs**: Inflating the value of insured property to obtain higher coverage. An example could be a homeowner inflating the value of their home and contents to receive a larger payout in case of a claim.
- **Providing False Information**: Submitting incorrect or misleading information about the insured. For instance, a policyholder might lie about their health condition to obtain a life insurance policy at a lower premium.

5. Organized Fraud

In recent years, organized crime syndicates have increasingly targeted the Indian insurance industry. These groups often employ sophisticated techniques, including:

- **Claim Rings**: Creating fake claims through a network of individuals. For example, a group might stage multiple car accidents involving different members to claim insurance money.
- **Doctor Shopping**: Seeking multiple doctors to obtain unnecessary medical tests and treatments. An example

could be a policyholder visiting several doctors to get multiple prescriptions and claim reimbursement for all.

- **Vehicle Cloning**: Creating duplicate vehicles for fraudulent claims. For instance, fraudsters might use a cloned vehicle to stage an accident and claim insurance money for both the original and the cloned vehicle.

6. Cybercrime

With the increasing reliance on technology, cybercrime has emerged as a significant threat to the insurance industry. Cybercriminals target insurers and policyholders alike, through:

- **Data Breaches**: Stealing sensitive customer information for fraudulent purposes. For example, hackers might steal personal information from an insurance company's database to file false claims.
- **Phishing Attacks**: Deceiving individuals into revealing personal information. An example could be sending fake emails that appear to be from an insurance company, tricking policyholders into providing their login credentials.
- **Cyber Extortion**: Threatening to expose sensitive data unless a ransom is paid. For instance, cybercriminals might threaten to release confidential customer information unless the insurance company pays a ransom.

7. Insurance Agent Fraud

Unfortunately, some insurance agents are involved in fraudulent activities, such as:

- **Mis-selling Policies**: Selling unsuitable policies to customers. For example, an agent might sell a high-premium policy to a customer who does not need such extensive coverage.
- **Misappropriation of Premiums**: Misusing customer premiums for personal gain. An example could be an agent pocketing the premiums paid by policyholders instead of forwarding them to the insurance company.
- **Collusion with Claimants**: Assisting policyholders in filing fraudulent claims. For instance, an agent might help a policyholder fabricate a claim for a non-existent loss.

Addressing Insurance Fraud

Addressing insurance fraud in India requires a multi-pronged approach involving insurers, regulators, law enforcement agencies, and the public. This includes strengthening fraud detection systems, enhancing investigative capabilities, imposing stricter penalties for fraudsters, and promoting awareness among policyholders. By working together, these stakeholders can create a more secure and trustworthy insurance environment.

CHAPTER THREE

Deep Dive into Specific Fraud Types: Inflated Insurance Claims

Inflated insurance claims occur when individuals or businesses exaggerate the extent of a loss or damage to receive a higher payout than they are entitled to. This form of insurance fraud significantly impacts premiums for honest policyholders and undermines the integrity of the insurance industry.

Common Examples of Inflated Claims

Auto Insurance

- **Exaggerated Injury Claims:** Claiming severe whiplash or other injuries from a minor accident. For example, a minor fender-bender might result in a claim for debilitating back pain, requiring extensive and costly medical treatment.
- **Inflated Repair Costs:** Providing estimates from fraudulent repair shops or claiming non-existent damages. An example could be a policyholder colluding with a repair shop to inflate the cost of repairs, such as

replacing parts that were not damaged.

- **Staged Accidents**: Colluding with others to create a fake accident and file claims for injuries and property damage. For instance, a group of individuals might stage a collision at a low speed, ensuring minimal actual damage but claiming extensive injuries and vehicle repairs.

Homeowners Insurance

- **Padding Inventory Lists**: Claiming items that were never owned or overstating the value of possessions. For example, after a burglary, a homeowner might claim that expensive electronics and jewelry were stolen, even if they never owned such items.
- **Inflated Repair Costs**: Exaggerating the extent of damage to a home or its contents. An example could be a homeowner claiming that a minor water leak caused extensive structural damage, requiring costly repairs.
- **Arson**: Intentionally setting fire to a property to collect insurance proceeds. For instance, a business owner facing financial difficulties might set fire to their premises to claim the insurance money.

Health Insurance

- **Phantom Billing**: Charging for services that were never provided. For example, a healthcare provider might bill an insurance company for treatments or procedures that were never performed on the patient.
- **Up-coding**: Billing for a more expensive procedure than was actually performed. An example could be a doctor performing a simple procedure but billing for a more

complex and costly one.

- **Unnecessary Medical Tests**: Ordering tests that are not medically necessary. For instance, a doctor might order a series of expensive diagnostic tests for a patient without any medical justification, solely to increase the insurance payout.

Business Insurance

- **Inflated Business Income Loss**: Overstating the financial impact of a business interruption. For example, a business might claim that a temporary closure due to a minor incident resulted in significant financial losses, far exceeding the actual impact.
- **False Claims for Property Damage**: Exaggerating the extent of damage to business property. An example could be a business owner claiming that a minor incident, such as a small fire, caused extensive damage to equipment and inventory.

How Inflated Claims Affect You

- **Increased Premiums**: Insurance companies pass the cost of fraudulent claims onto policyholders through higher premiums. This means that honest policyholders end up paying more for their insurance coverage.
- **Reduced Payouts**: As insurance companies become more vigilant in detecting fraud, legitimate claims may be scrutinized more closely, potentially leading to delayed or reduced payouts. This can be frustrating for policyholders who have genuine claims.
- **Weakened Insurance Industry**: Widespread insurance fraud can destabilize the insurance industry, limiting

coverage options for consumers. This can result in fewer choices and higher costs for insurance products.

By understanding the various forms of inflated insurance claims and their impact, both insurers and policyholders can work together to combat fraud and maintain the integrity of the insurance system.

Investigators look for several red flags when identifying inflated insurance claims. These indicators help them determine whether a claim might be fraudulent and warrant further investigation. Here are some common red flags:

Red Flags in Auto Insurance Claims

- **Inconsistent Damage**: The damage reported does not match the description of the accident. For example, minor collisions resulting in extensive damage claims.
- **Excessive Medical Treatment**: Claims for severe injuries from minor accidents, especially when the medical treatment seems disproportionate to the accident's severity.
- **Frequent Claims**: The policyholder has a history of filing multiple claims, particularly for similar types of accidents or damages.
- **Suspicious Repair Estimates**: Estimates from repair shops that are unusually high or come from shops with a history of fraudulent activity.

Red Flags in Homeowners Insurance Claims

- **Overstated Inventory**: The claimed value of lost or damaged items is significantly higher than their actual worth or includes items that were never owned.

- **Recent Policy Changes**: Significant increases in coverage shortly before a claim is filed, especially for high-value items.
- **Delayed Reporting**: The claim is reported long after the alleged incident, which can indicate an attempt to fabricate or exaggerate the loss.
- **Unusual Circumstances**: The circumstances of the loss are unusual or inconsistent with typical claims, such as a fire starting in an unlikely location.

Red Flags in Health Insurance Claims

- **Excessive Billing**: Bills for treatments or procedures that seem excessive or unnecessary, such as multiple diagnostic tests for a minor condition.
- **Inconsistent Medical Records**: Discrepancies between the medical records and the claimed treatments or procedures.
- **Frequent Provider Changes**: The policyholder frequently changes healthcare providers, which can indicate "doctor shopping" for unnecessary treatments.
- **Unusual Treatment Patterns**: Patterns of treatment that do not align with standard medical practices, such as repeated procedures that are not medically justified.

Red Flags in Business Insurance Claims

- **Inflated Losses**: Claims for business interruption or property damage that seem exaggerated compared to the actual impact.
- **Unverified Documentation**: Lack of supporting documentation for the claimed losses, such as missing receipts or invoices.

- **Financial Difficulties**: The business was experiencing financial difficulties before the claim, which can indicate a motive for fraud.
- **Unusual Timing**: The claim is filed shortly after the policy was purchased or significantly increased in coverage.

General Red Flags Across All Insurance Types

- **Inconsistent Statements**: Discrepancies between the policyholder's statements and the evidence or witness accounts.
- **Reluctance to Provide Information**: The policyholder is hesitant or refuses to provide necessary information or documentation.
- **Unusual Behavior**: The policyholder exhibits unusual behavior, such as being overly eager to settle the claim quickly.
- **Third-Party Involvement**: Involvement of third parties, such as repair shops or medical providers, with a history of fraudulent activity.

By being vigilant and looking for these red flags, investigators can identify potentially inflated claims and take appropriate action to prevent fraud.

Case Study: The Staged Accident Ring
Background

In a bustling metropolitan area, an insurance company noticed an unusual spike in auto insurance claims. Many of these claims involved minor accidents but resulted in substantial injury claims and high repair costs. The pattern was suspicious, prompting the company to initiate a deeper investigation.

Red Flags
Several red flags were identified:

1. **Frequent Claims**: Multiple claims were filed by the same individuals or groups of individuals within a short period.
2. **Inconsistent Damage**: The reported damage to the vehicles did not match the descriptions of the accidents. Minor collisions were resulting in claims for extensive repairs.
3. **Excessive Medical Treatment**: The injury claims were disproportionately high compared to the severity of the accidents. Claimants were reporting severe injuries like whiplash and back pain from low-speed collisions.
4. **Suspicious Repair Shops**: The repair estimates were coming from a small number of repair shops, all of which had a history of inflated estimates.

Investigation
The insurance company's fraud investigation unit decided to conduct surveillance and gather more evidence. They installed hidden cameras near the repair shops and monitored the activities of the claimants.

Findings
The investigation revealed a well-organized fraud ring:

- **Staged Accidents**: The claimants were staging accidents with the help of accomplices. They would deliberately cause minor collisions in low-traffic areas to avoid detection.
- **Collusion with Repair Shops**: The repair shops were in on the scheme, providing inflated repair estimates and sometimes billing for repairs that were never

performed.

- **Medical Fraud**: Some medical providers were also involved, diagnosing claimants with severe injuries and prescribing unnecessary treatments to inflate the medical bills.

Outcome

With the evidence gathered, the insurance company was able to:

- **Deny Fraudulent Claims**: They denied the fraudulent claims, saving millions of dollars in potential payouts.
- **Prosecute the Fraudsters**: The evidence was handed over to law enforcement, leading to the arrest and prosecution of several individuals involved in the fraud ring.
- **Implement Preventive Measures**: The company strengthened its fraud detection systems and implemented stricter verification processes for claims.

This case highlights the importance of vigilance and thorough investigation in uncovering insurance fraud. By identifying red flags and taking proactive measures, the insurance company was able to protect itself and its honest policyholders from the financial impact of fraud[1].

CHAPTER FOUR

Auto Insurance Fraud: Specific Examples and Challenges

Auto insurance fraud is a pervasive issue that costs the insurance industry billions of dollars annually. It involves deception or misrepresentation to obtain an insurance benefit or avoid paying a premium. Here are some specific examples and the challenges associated with auto insurance fraud.

Types of Auto Insurance Fraud

Soft Fraud

Soft fraud involves exaggerating a claim or providing false information to inflate the claim amount.

- **Exaggerated Injuries**: Claiming more severe injuries than actually sustained in an accident. For example, a minor fender-bender might lead to claims of severe whiplash and chronic back pain, requiring extensive and costly medical treatment.
- **Inflated Repair Costs**: Providing estimates from fraudulent repair shops or claiming non-existent

damages. An example could be a policyholder colluding with a repair shop to inflate the cost of repairs, such as replacing parts that were not damaged.

- **Padding Claims**: Adding extra items or services to a claim that were not actually damaged or needed. For instance, a claimant might include unrelated repairs or maintenance work in the insurance claim.

Hard Fraud

Hard fraud involves more elaborate schemes to defraud insurance companies.

- **Staged Accidents**: Colluding with others to create a fake accident and file claims for injuries and property damage. For example, a group of individuals might stage a collision at a low speed, ensuring minimal actual damage but claiming extensive injuries and vehicle repairs.
- **Vehicle Theft and Burning**: Stealing or burning a vehicle to collect insurance proceeds. An example could be a policyholder reporting their car stolen and later found burned, when in reality, they orchestrated the theft and arson.
- **Ghost Driving**: Claiming someone else was driving the vehicle at the time of an accident to avoid higher premiums. For instance, a policyholder might claim that a friend or relative was driving during an accident to avoid a premium increase.
- **Premium Fraud**: Providing false information on an insurance application to obtain a lower premium. An example could be underreporting the number of miles driven annually or the primary location where the vehicle is kept.

Impact of Auto Insurance Fraud

- **Increased Premiums**: The costs of fraudulent claims are passed on to all policyholders in the form of higher premiums. This means that honest policyholders end up paying more for their insurance coverage.
- **Weakened Insurance Industry**: Widespread fraud can destabilize the insurance industry, leading to fewer coverage options and higher costs for consumers. This can result in fewer choices and higher costs for insurance products.
- **Legal Consequences**: Auto insurance fraud is a serious crime with potential penalties including fines and imprisonment. Those caught committing fraud can face significant legal repercussions.

Prevention and Detection

Insurance companies employ various methods to detect fraud, including:

- **Claim Analysis**: Detailed review of claims for inconsistencies or red flags. For example, comparing the damage reported with the accident description to identify discrepancies.
- **Fraud Investigation Units**: Specialized teams dedicated to investigating suspicious claims. These units use various techniques, such as surveillance and interviews, to uncover fraudulent activities.
- **Data Analytics**: Using advanced data analysis techniques to identify patterns of fraud. For instance, analyzing claims data to detect unusual patterns, such as frequent claims from the same individuals or repair shops.

- **Cooperation with Law Enforcement**: Working with law enforcement agencies to prosecute fraudsters. This collaboration helps ensure that those committing fraud are held accountable.

Consumer Role in Preventing Fraud

As a consumer, you can help prevent auto insurance fraud by:

- **Being Honest on Your Insurance Application**: Providing accurate information about your driving habits, vehicle usage, and other relevant details.
- **Providing Accurate Information When Filing a Claim**: Ensuring that all information provided in a claim is truthful and accurate.
- **Obtaining Multiple Repair Estimates**: Before approving work, get multiple estimates to ensure that the repair costs are reasonable and justified.
- **Reporting Suspicious Activity**: If you suspect fraudulent activity, report it to your insurance company. This helps protect the integrity of the insurance system.

By understanding the various forms of auto insurance fraud and the challenges associated with detecting and preventing it, both insurers and policyholders can work together to combat fraud and maintain the integrity of the insurance system.

CHAPTER FIVE

Third-Party Insurance Claims: A Comprehensive Overview

Understanding Third-Party Insurance

In India, third-party insurance is mandatory for all motor vehicles. This type of insurance covers damages or injuries caused to a third party by your vehicle. Essentially, if you cause an accident, the insurance will cover the costs incurred by the other person involved, such as medical expenses, property damage, or loss of life.

Types of Third-Party Claims

There are primarily two types of third-party claims:

1. **Bodily Injury**: This covers injuries sustained by a third party due to an accident caused by your vehicle. It includes medical expenses, loss of income, and disability benefits. For example, if you hit a pedestrian and they suffer injuries, their medical bills and loss of income would be covered under your third-party

insurance.

2. **Property Damage**: This covers damages caused to a third party's property due to an accident caused by your vehicle. This includes damage to other vehicles, buildings, or any other property. For instance, if you collide with another car and cause damage to their vehicle, the repair costs would be covered under your third-party insurance.

The Claim Process

1. **Reporting the Accident**: Immediately after the accident, inform the police and obtain a First Information Report (FIR). Also, gather details of the other party involved, including their contact information and vehicle details.
2. **Inform Your Insurer**: Contact your insurance company and inform them about the accident, providing all necessary details.
3. **Claim Filing**: The injured party or the owner of the damaged property can file a claim with the insurance company of the vehicle that caused the accident.
4. **Investigation**: The insurance company will investigate the claim to verify the details and assess the damages.
5. **Settlement**: If the claim is valid, the insurance company will settle the claim by paying compensation to the third party.

Important Points to Remember

- **Mandatory Coverage**: Third-party insurance is compulsory in India. Driving without it is illegal and can result in hefty fines and legal consequences.

- **Claim Limits**: The coverage amount under third-party insurance is determined by the policy. It's essential to have adequate coverage to protect yourself from financial liabilities.
- **Timely Claims**: It's crucial to file a claim as soon as possible after the accident to avoid delays and complications.
- **Legal Assistance**: In case of disputes or complex claims, it's advisable to consult with a legal professional to navigate the process effectively.

Example Scenario

Imagine you are driving your car and accidentally hit another car at a traffic signal. The other car is damaged, and the driver sustains minor injuries. In this case, the other driver can file a third-party insurance claim with your insurance company to cover the repair costs of their car and their medical expenses.

Note

While third-party insurance covers damages caused to others, it does not cover damages to your own vehicle. For that, you need comprehensive insurance.

Unique Aspects of Third-Party Insurance Fraud in India

Third-party insurance fraud in India has some unique characteristics due to the socio-economic and regulatory environment. Here are some specific examples and challenges:

1. **False Injury Claims**: Fraudsters may exaggerate or fabricate injuries to claim higher compensation. For instance, a minor accident might lead to claims of severe injuries requiring long-term medical treatment.

2. **Staged Accidents**: Individuals may stage accidents to claim insurance money. This often involves collusion between the claimant and witnesses or even medical professionals who provide false injury reports.
3. **Phantom Claims**: Claims made for accidents that never occurred. Fraudsters might file claims using fake accident reports and witness statements.
4. **Collusion with Repair Shops**: Some repair shops may inflate repair costs or bill for repairs that were never performed, splitting the proceeds with the claimant.
5. **Document Forgery**: Fraudsters may forge documents such as medical reports, police FIRs, and repair bills to support their false claims.

Challenges in Detecting and Preventing Fraud

- **Verification Difficulties**: Verifying the authenticity of claims can be challenging, especially in cases involving staged accidents or false injury claims.
- **Resource Constraints**: Insurance companies may lack the resources to thoroughly investigate every claim, leading to some fraudulent claims slipping through the cracks.
- **Legal Hurdles**: Proving fraud in court can be difficult, requiring substantial evidence and legal expertise.

Prevention and Detection Strategies

- **Enhanced Verification**: Implementing stricter verification processes for claims, including cross-checking documents and conducting thorough investigations.

- **Data Analytics**: Using advanced data analytics to identify patterns and anomalies that may indicate fraud.
- **Collaboration with Authorities**: Working closely with law enforcement agencies to investigate and prosecute fraudsters.
- **Public Awareness**: Educating policyholders about the consequences of fraud and encouraging them to report suspicious activities.

By understanding third-party insurance and the claim process, as well as the unique aspects of fraud in the Indian context, you can better protect yourself from financial losses and contribute to a more transparent and fair insurance system.

CHAPTER SIX

Own Damage Claims: A Potential Minefield – Exploring frauds within Property and Vehicle Insurance

Unlike third-party claims, which primarily involve damages caused to others, own damage claims pertain to losses incurred by the insured themselves. While these claims might seem less prone to fraud, they can still be a target for unscrupulous individuals.

The Nature of Own Damage Claims

Own damage claims arise when an insured vehicle is damaged due to accidents, theft, fire, or natural calamities. The insurer is obligated to compensate the insured for the financial loss incurred. These claims cover a wide range of incidents, from minor scratches to total loss of the vehicle.

Threats Contained Within Own Damage Claims

While not as prevalent as third-party fraud, own damage claims also present opportunities for deception. Here are some common types of fraud associated with own damage claims:

1. Inflated Repair Costs

- **Exaggerated Damage**: Claiming more extensive damage than actually occurred. For example, a minor scratch on a car might be claimed as a deep dent requiring extensive bodywork.
- **Phantom Parts**: Billing for parts that were not replaced. An example could be a repair shop charging for a new bumper when the original was simply repaired.
- **Unnecessary Repairs**: Claiming repairs that were not required. For instance, a policyholder might claim that the entire engine needs replacement when only a minor part was damaged.

2. Staged Accidents

- **Creating a False Accident Scenario**: Deliberately causing an accident to claim insurance benefits. For example, a vehicle owner might stage a collision with a stationary object to claim insurance for damages.
- **Colluding with Others**: Working with accomplices to cause damage to the vehicle. An example could be two drivers colluding to stage a collision and then filing claims for the damages.

3. Theft and Recovery Fraud

- **Filing a False Theft Claim**: Reporting a vehicle as stolen and later recovering it without informing the insurance company. For instance, a vehicle owner might report their car as stolen, only to recover it a few days later without notifying the insurer.

- **Colluding with Thieves**: Staging a theft and recovering the vehicle for a share of the insurance payout. An example could be a vehicle owner working with a thief to fake a theft and then splitting the insurance money.

4. Vehicle Modification Fraud

- **Unauthorized Modifications**: Making unauthorized modifications to a vehicle and then claiming compensation for damage to the modified parts. For example, installing aftermarket parts without informing the insurer and then claiming compensation for damage to these parts in an accident.

5. Total Loss Fraud

- **Claiming a Total Loss**: Declaring a vehicle as a total loss when it can be repaired. For instance, a vehicle with minor damage might be claimed as a total loss to receive a higher payout.
- **Under-reporting Salvage Value**: Providing a lower salvage value for the vehicle to increase the insurance payout. An example could be a policyholder undervaluing the salvageable parts of a damaged vehicle.

Challenges in Detecting Own Damage Fraud

- **Lack of Clear Evidence**: Unlike third-party claims, where there are often multiple parties involved, own damage claims primarily rely on the insured's statements and supporting documents. This makes it challenging to verify the authenticity of the claims.

- **Complexity of Vehicle Valuation**: Determining the actual value of a damaged vehicle can be complex, especially for high-end or older models. This complexity can be exploited by fraudsters to inflate claims.
- **Collusion with Repair Shops**: Fraudsters often work in collusion with repair shops to inflate repair costs. This collusion can make it difficult for insurers to detect fraudulent activities.

Countermeasures

To mitigate the risk of own damage fraud, insurance companies can implement the following measures:

- **Thorough Vehicle Inspections**: Conducting detailed inspections of damaged vehicles to identify inconsistencies. This can help in detecting exaggerated or false claims.
- **Data Analytics**: Using data to identify patterns of fraudulent claims. Advanced analytics can help in spotting anomalies and trends that indicate potential fraud.
- **Anti-fraud Software**: Employing software to detect anomalies in claims data. These tools can flag suspicious claims for further investigation.
- **Collaboration with Repair Shops**: Building strong relationships with repair shops to detect fraudulent activities. Trusted partnerships can help in ensuring that repair estimates are accurate and justified.
- **Customer Education**: Informing policyholders about the consequences of insurance fraud. Educated

customers are less likely to engage in fraudulent activities and more likely to report suspicious behavior.

By combining these efforts, insurance companies can enhance their ability to detect and prevent own damage fraud, protecting both their financial interests and the integrity of the insurance system.

CHAPTER SEVEN

Unraveling the Deception: Understanding Inflated Repair Claims

Inflated repair costs are a prevalent form of insurance fraud in India. This occurs when repair shops or individuals exaggerate the extent of damage to a vehicle to claim a higher compensation amount from the insurance company. Think of it as a magician's trick, where the illusion of damage is far greater than the reality.

Common Tactics Used to Inflate Repair Costs

1. Phantom Parts

- **Claiming Replacement of Parts That Were Never Actually Damaged or Replaced:** This is akin to a chef charging you for a gourmet meal but serving you a simple sandwich instead.

  - **Example:** A repair shop might claim to have replaced an entire engine block when only minor repairs were necessary. Imagine being billed for a brand-new engine when all that was needed was a spark plug change.

2. Exaggerated Labor Costs

- **Overstating the Number of Labor Hours Required for Repairs**: This is like a painter charging you for a mural when all they did was touch up a small spot.

  - **Example**: A simple dent repair might be billed as a complex bodywork job requiring multiple labor hours. Picture a tiny scratch on your car being treated as if the entire side needed to be rebuilt.

3. Substandard Parts

- **Using Low-Quality or Second-Hand Parts and Charging for Original Equipment Manufacturer (OEM) Parts**: This is similar to buying a designer dress but receiving a cheap knockoff.

  - **Example**: Replacing original car parts with aftermarket parts of inferior quality but billing for the cost of OEM parts. Imagine paying for a high-end stereo system but getting a basic, low-quality one instead.

4. Unnecessary Repairs

- **Recommending and Performing Repairs That Are Not Required to Restore the Vehicle to Its Pre-Accident Condition**: This is like a doctor prescribing surgery for a simple cold.

- ◦ **Example**: Suggesting a complete paint job for a vehicle with minor scratches. Think of being told your entire house needs repainting when only a small patch needs touch-up.

5. Collusion with Surveyors

- **Repair Shops Often Collude with Insurance Surveyors to Inflate Repair Estimates**: This is akin to a referee being bribed to favor one team over another in a sports match.

  - ◦ **Example**: A surveyor might overlook discrepancies in repair estimates in exchange for financial benefits. Imagine an umpire ignoring a clear foul because they've been paid off.

Challenges in Detecting Inflated Repair Costs

- **Lack of Standardized Repair Costs**: There is no uniform pricing system for auto repairs in India, making it difficult to assess the reasonableness of repair estimates. It's like trying to compare apples to oranges without a common standard.
- **Complex Vehicle Systems**: Modern vehicles have intricate components and systems, making it challenging for non-experts to verify the necessity of certain repairs. This complexity can be exploited by fraudsters, much like a tech-savvy person taking advantage of someone who isn't familiar with gadgets.

- **Geographical Variations**: Repair costs can vary significantly between urban and rural areas, making it difficult to establish benchmarks. It's like the cost of living being vastly different in a big city compared to a small town.
- **Trust in Repair Shops**: Many vehicle owners rely on the recommendations of their regular repair shops, making them vulnerable to inflated bills. This trust can be misplaced, much like trusting a friend who turns out to be deceitful.

Countermeasures

To combat inflated repair costs, insurance companies can implement the following measures:

- **Independent Assessments**: Hiring independent assessors to verify the extent of damage and the reasonableness of repair estimates. This is like getting a second opinion from a different doctor to ensure the diagnosis is accurate.
- **Repair Cost Databases**: Creating databases of average repair costs for different vehicle models and types of damage. This can serve as a benchmark, much like having a price guide for various products.
- **Auditing Repair Shops**: Conducting regular audits of repair shops to identify fraudulent practices. This is akin to financial audits that ensure businesses are not engaging in deceptive practices.
- **Customer Education**: Informing policyholders about their rights and encouraging them to obtain multiple repair estimates. Knowledge is power, much like knowing your consumer rights can protect you from scams.

- **Collaboration with Law Enforcement**: Working with law enforcement agencies to investigate and prosecute cases of fraud. This partnership is crucial, much like the collaboration between police and community members to prevent crime.

By combining these efforts, insurance companies can enhance their ability to detect and prevent inflated repair costs, ensuring a fair and transparent process for all policyholders.

CHAPTER EIGHT

Staged Accidents: A Growing Menace- Examining the Modus Operandi of Staged Accidents

Staged accidents are a serious form of insurance fraud where individuals deliberately cause accidents to claim insurance benefits. These incidents involve a calculated plan to deceive insurance companies and reap financial gains. Think of it as a theatrical performance where every move is choreographed to perfection, but the audience (insurance companies) is unaware that they are being duped.

Common Types of Staged Accidents

1. Rear-End Collisions

- **Description**: This is the most common type of staged accident, where one vehicle intentionally collides with another from behind. The impact is usually minor, but the occupants of the vehicle that was hit often claim whiplash or other injuries.

- **Example**: Imagine a car suddenly braking at a green light, causing the vehicle behind to rear-end it. The driver and passengers of the front car then claim severe neck and back injuries, despite the minor impact.

2. Swerving Accidents

- **Description**: In this scenario, one vehicle deliberately swerves into another, causing minor damage but claiming significant injuries.
- **Example**: Picture a car swerving into another lane without warning, causing a side-swipe collision. The driver of the swerving car then claims extensive injuries and vehicle damage, even though the actual impact was minimal.

3. Pedestrian Accidents

- **Description**: These involve staged accidents involving pedestrians who are often in collusion with the driver.
- **Example**: A pedestrian might suddenly step in front of a slow-moving car, pretending to be hit. The pedestrian and the driver then file claims for injuries and damages, splitting the insurance payout.

4. Vehicle Theft and Recovery

- **Description**: A vehicle is stolen and then recovered with fabricated damage to claim insurance for repairs or total loss.

- **Example**: A car owner might report their vehicle as stolen, only to recover it later with intentional damage. They then claim insurance for the supposed theft and the fabricated damage.

Examples of Staged Accidents in India

- **Organized Rings**: In some cases, organized groups of individuals are involved in staging accidents, with multiple vehicles and participants. These rings operate like well-oiled machines, with each member playing a specific role in the fraud.
- **Involvement of Repair Shops**: Repair shops often collaborate with fraudsters to create fake accident scenarios and inflate repair costs. They might provide inflated repair estimates or bill for repairs that were never performed.
- **Exploitation of Vulnerable Sections**: People from economically weaker sections are sometimes lured into participating in staged accidents for financial gain. They are promised a share of the insurance payout in exchange for their participation.

The Impact of Staged Accidents

Staged accidents have a significant impact on the insurance industry and society as a whole:

- **Increased Insurance Premiums**: The cost of fraudulent claims is ultimately borne by honest policyholders through increased premiums. It's like everyone having to pay more for a meal because a few people decided to dine and dash.

- **Weakened Insurance Industry**: Widespread fraud can erode trust in the insurance industry, leading to financial instability. This is akin to termites slowly eating away at the foundation of a house.
- **Distorted Claims Data**: Staged accidents can skew insurance claims data, making it difficult to accurately assess risk and set premiums. It's like trying to solve a puzzle with pieces that don't fit.
- **Resource Wastage**: Law enforcement and insurance companies invest significant resources in investigating fraudulent claims. This is like firefighters having to put out a fire that was intentionally set.

Challenges in Detecting Staged Accidents

- **Lack of Evidence**: In many cases, there is limited physical evidence to prove that an accident was staged. It's like trying to catch a ghost.
- **Collusion**: Fraudsters often work in collusion with witnesses, medical professionals, and repair shops to create a convincing story. This makes it difficult to unravel the web of deceit.
- **Complex Investigation**: Uncovering the truth behind a staged accident requires extensive investigation and analysis. It's like peeling an onion, with each layer revealing more complexity.

Countermeasures

Insurance companies employ various methods to detect staged accidents:

- **Data Analysis**: Analyzing claim patterns to identify suspicious trends. This is like using a magnifying glass to spot hidden details.

- **Risk Assessment**: Evaluating the risk profile of policyholders and vehicles. This helps in identifying high-risk individuals who might be more likely to commit fraud.
- **Surveillance**: Using surveillance to gather evidence of suspicious behavior. This is akin to having a detective on the case, watching for any signs of foul play.
- **Collaboration with Law Enforcement**: Working with law enforcement agencies to investigate and prosecute fraudsters. This partnership is crucial in bringing fraudsters to justice.

While these measures can help to deter staged accidents, it is a continuous battle that requires vigilance and innovation from the insurance industry. By staying one step ahead of the fraudsters, insurance companies can protect themselves and their policyholders from the financial impact of staged accidents.

CHAPTER NINE

Theft and Recovery Fraud: A Deceptive Scheme – Understanding the Intricacies of Vehicle Theft-Related Fraud

Theft and recovery fraud is a form of insurance fraud where a vehicle is stolen and subsequently recovered with fabricated damage. The insured then claims compensation from the insurance company for the alleged damages. This type of fraud is like a well-rehearsed play, where every actor knows their role, but the audience (insurance companies) is unaware of the deception.

Common Modus Operandi

1. Staged Theft

- **Description**: In some cases, the vehicle owner colludes with thieves to stage a theft. The vehicle is hidden for a predetermined period and then "recovered" with fabricated damage.
- **Example**: Imagine a car owner working with a thief to "steal" their vehicle. The car is hidden in a garage for a few weeks, during which minor damages are intentionally inflicted. The car is then "found" and returned to the owner, who files a claim for extensive repairs.

2. Accidental Recovery

- **Description**: In other instances, a stolen vehicle might be recovered by the police with accidental damage. The owner, unaware of the damage, files a claim for the full extent of the damage.
- **Example**: A car is genuinely stolen and later recovered by the police with some scratches and dents. The owner, seeing an opportunity, exaggerates the damage when filing the insurance claim, claiming that the vehicle is in much worse condition than it actually is.

3. Inflated Repair Costs

- **Description**: Even if the theft is genuine, the owner or repair shop might inflate the cost of repairs to maximize the insurance claim.
- **Example**: After a genuine theft and recovery, the repair shop might bill for high-end parts and extensive labor, even though only minor repairs were needed. The owner and the repair shop split the extra money from the inflated claim.

Examples of Theft and Recovery Fraud
1. Fake Accident Scenario

- **Description**: A stolen vehicle is involved in a staged accident to create the appearance of significant damage.
- **Example**: A car reported as stolen is later found crashed into a tree. The owner claims that the thieves caused the accident, leading to major structural damage. In reality, the accident was staged to inflate the insurance claim.

2. Exaggerated Damage

- **Description**: Minor scratches or dents are claimed as major structural damage.
- **Example**: A car recovered with a few minor scratches is claimed to have severe body damage, requiring extensive and costly repairs. The owner might even replace undamaged parts to make the damage seem more severe.

3. Replacement of Parts

- **Description**: Original parts are replaced with cheaper alternatives, but the insurance company is billed for the cost of original parts.
- **Example**: A car's original, high-quality tires are replaced with cheaper ones, but the insurance claim includes the cost of the original tires. The owner and the repair shop pocket the difference.

Challenges in Detection

- **Lack of Evidence**: Proving that a theft was staged or that damage was fabricated can be challenging due to the lack of evidence. It's like trying to solve a mystery with missing clues.
- **Collusion**: Fraudsters often work in collusion with thieves, tow truck drivers, and repair shops to create a convincing story. This network of deceit makes it difficult to uncover the truth.
- **Time Lapse**: The time between the theft and recovery can make it difficult to verify the extent of the damage. Over time, evidence can be lost or tampered with, complicating the investigation.

Countermeasures

Insurance companies employ various methods to detect theft and recovery fraud:

- **Vehicle Tracking Devices**: Using GPS tracking to monitor vehicle movement and identify suspicious activity. This technology can help track the vehicle's location and movements, providing crucial evidence in case of a suspected fraud.
- **Data Analysis**: Analyzing claim patterns to identify anomalies. Advanced data analytics can reveal unusual patterns, such as frequent claims from the same individuals or repair shops, indicating potential fraud.
- **Inspection of Recovered Vehicles**: Conducting thorough inspections of recovered vehicles to assess the extent of damage. Detailed inspections can help identify inconsistencies between the reported damage and the actual condition of the vehicle.
- **Collaboration with Law Enforcement**: Working with law enforcement agencies to investigate suspicious

cases. This partnership is essential for gathering evidence and prosecuting fraudsters.

By understanding the intricacies of theft and recovery fraud and implementing effective countermeasures, insurance companies can better protect themselves and their policyholders from this deceptive scheme.

CHAPTER TEN

Vehicle Modification Fraud: A Risky Endeavor - Fraud Involving Vehicle Alterations

Vehicle modification fraud occurs when a vehicle owner makes unauthorized changes to their vehicle and then files a claim for damages to these modified parts. This type of fraud is often perpetrated to gain financial benefits from the insurance company. It's like dressing up a car in a fancy costume and then pretending it was always that way to get a bigger payout.

Common Types of Vehicle Modifications

1. Performance Enhancements

- **Description**: Modifications that increase a vehicle's speed, acceleration, or handling.

- **Examples**: Engine tuning, turbochargers, performance exhaust systems. Imagine a car owner installing a turbocharger to boost speed but not informing the insurer.

2. Aesthetic Modifications

- **Description**: Changes made to the appearance of a vehicle.
- **Examples**: Body kits, spoilers, custom paint jobs, aftermarket wheels. Think of a car with a flashy new body kit and custom paint job that the insurer knows nothing about.

3. Interior Modifications

- **Description**: Alterations to the vehicle's interior.
- **Examples**: Custom seats, audio systems, upgraded electronics. Picture a car with a high-end audio system and custom leather seats that were never reported to the insurance company.

How Vehicle Modification Fraud Works
1. Unreported Modifications

- **Description**: Vehicle owners often fail to inform their insurance company about modifications made to their vehicles.
- **Example**: A car owner installs a high-performance engine but does not disclose it to the insurance company. When the car is involved in an accident, the owner claims compensation for the damaged engine, including the cost of the performance modifications.

2. Inflated Claim Values

- **Description**: When the modified vehicle is involved in an accident, owners claim compensation for the damaged modified parts at inflated prices.
- **Example**: A vehicle with a custom paint job is involved in a minor accident. The owner claims the entire cost of repainting the vehicle, including the cost of the custom paint job.

3. Claiming Original Parts

- **Description**: In some cases, owners claim that the damaged parts were original equipment manufacturer (OEM) parts, even though they were aftermarket modifications.
- **Example**: An aftermarket audio system is installed in a car. The owner fails to disclose the modification. When the car is stolen, the owner claims compensation for the stolen audio system as if it were an OEM part.

Examples of Vehicle Modification Fraud

- **High-Performance Engine**: A car owner installs a high-performance engine but does not disclose it to the insurance company. When the car is involved in an accident, the owner claims compensation for the damaged engine, including the cost of the performance modifications.
- **Custom Paint Job**: A vehicle with a custom paint job is involved in a minor accident. The owner claims the entire cost of repainting the vehicle, including the cost of the custom paint job.

- **Aftermarket Audio System**: An aftermarket audio system is installed in a car. The owner fails to disclose the modification. When the car is stolen, the owner claims compensation for the stolen audio system.

Challenges in Detecting Vehicle Modification Fraud

- **Lack of Disclosure**: Many vehicle owners are unaware of the requirement to disclose modifications to their insurance company. This lack of awareness can lead to unintentional fraud.
- **Difficulty in Assessing Modifications**: Determining the value of aftermarket parts and the impact of modifications on a vehicle's overall value can be challenging. It's like trying to appraise a house with hidden renovations.
- **Collusion with Repair Shops**: Repair shops might collude with vehicle owners to inflate the cost of repairs for modified parts. This collusion can make it difficult to detect fraudulent claims.

Countermeasures

To mitigate the risk of vehicle modification fraud, insurance companies can implement the following measures:

- **Clear Disclosure Requirements**: Clearly communicate the requirement for policyholders to disclose vehicle modifications. This transparency can help prevent unintentional fraud.
- **Regular Policy Reviews**: Encourage policyholders to review their insurance coverage regularly to ensure it aligns with their vehicle's condition. Regular reviews

can catch modifications that need to be reported.

- **Vehicle Inspections**: Conduct periodic inspections of insured vehicles to identify unauthorized modifications. These inspections can help detect modifications that were not reported.
- **Data Analysis**: Use data analytics to identify patterns of suspicious claims related to modified vehicles. Advanced analytics can reveal trends and anomalies that indicate potential fraud.
- **Collaboration with Repair Shops**: Build strong relationships with repair shops to detect fraudulent claims. Trusted partnerships can help ensure that repair estimates are accurate and justified.

By understanding the intricacies of vehicle modification fraud and implementing effective countermeasures, insurance companies can better protect themselves and their policyholders from this risky endeavor.

CHAPTER ELEVEN

Total Loss Fraud: A Deceptive Practice – Understanding the Tactics Used to Defraud Insurance Companies in Total Loss Claims

A total loss occurs when the cost of repairing a damaged vehicle exceeds its insured value. In such cases, the insurance company declares the vehicle a total loss and compensates the owner for its value. However, this situation can be exploited by fraudulent individuals. Think of it as a magician's trick, where the illusion of a total loss is created to deceive the insurance company.

Common Types of Total Loss Fraud

1. Inflated Vehicle Value

- **Description**: Claiming a higher value for the vehicle than its actual market value by providing false or inflated purchase invoices.
- **Example**: A used car might be claimed as a newer model with a higher value. Imagine a 2010 model car being claimed as a 2018 model to get a higher payout. The owner might provide a fake invoice showing a recent purchase at a high price.

2. Underreporting Salvage Value

- **Description**: Claiming a lower salvage value for the damaged vehicle to increase the total loss claim amount by colluding with salvage yards.
- **Example**: A vehicle with significant salvage value might be claimed as having little or no value. For instance, a car that could be sold for parts at a decent price is reported as worthless, inflating the total loss claim.

3. Staged Accidents

- **Description**: Deliberately causing damage to a vehicle to claim a total loss, often involving minor accidents and exaggerating the damage.
- **Example**: A vehicle might be intentionally damaged in a minor collision to claim a total loss. Picture a car owner driving into a wall at low speed, causing just enough damage to make the car appear beyond repair.

4. Salvage Fraud

- **Description**: Selling the salvaged vehicle for a higher price than declared to the insurance company or keeping the vehicle for personal use after claiming a total loss.

- **Example**: A vehicle declared as a total loss might be repaired and sold without informing the insurance company. Imagine a car owner claiming a total loss, getting the payout, then fixing the car cheaply and selling it for a profit.

Challenges in Detecting Total Loss Fraud

- **Valuation Difficulties**: Determining the accurate value of a damaged vehicle can be complex, especially for older or modified vehicles. It's like trying to appraise a house with hidden renovations.
- **Lack of Transparency**: The process of valuing salvage vehicles is often opaque, making it difficult to verify the accuracy of salvage values. This lack of clarity can be exploited by fraudsters.
- **Collusion**: Fraudsters often work in collusion with salvage yards and repair shops to manipulate the process. This network of deceit makes it challenging to uncover the truth.

Countermeasures

Insurance companies can implement various measures to detect and prevent total loss fraud:

- **Independent Vehicle Valuations**: Hiring independent assessors to determine the actual value of the vehicle. This is like getting a second opinion from a different doctor to ensure the diagnosis is accurate.
- **Salvage Auctions**: Conducting transparent salvage auctions to obtain accurate market values. This

transparency can help prevent underreporting of salvage values.

- **Data Analytics**: Using data to identify patterns of suspicious total loss claims. Advanced analytics can reveal trends and anomalies that indicate potential fraud.
- **Investigative Tools**: Employing advanced technology to verify vehicle history and identify fraudulent activities. Tools like vehicle history reports can provide crucial information about past claims and repairs.
- **Collaboration with Law Enforcement**: Working with law enforcement agencies to investigate and prosecute fraudsters. This partnership is essential for gathering evidence and bringing fraudsters to justice.

By understanding the tactics used in total loss fraud and implementing effective countermeasures, insurance companies can better protect themselves and their policyholders from this deceptive practice.

CHAPTER TWELVE

Exaggerated Injury Claims: A Closer Look at Whiplash and Beyond – Focusing on Personal Injury Claims.

Exaggerated injury claims, particularly those involving whiplash, are a significant issue in the insurance industry. While whiplash is a genuine injury that can cause significant pain and suffering, it's also a condition that's often misused in fraudulent claims. Let's delve deeper into this issue, exploring the tactics used and the challenges faced by insurance companies.

Understanding Whiplash

Whiplash is a soft tissue injury to the neck caused by a sudden, forceful back-and-forth movement of the head. It often occurs in rear-end car collisions. Symptoms can include neck pain, stiffness, headaches, dizziness, and shoulder pain. Think of it as the neck being whipped back and forth, much like the cracking of a whip.

Exaggerating Whiplash Claims

The problem arises when individuals claim severe or long-lasting whiplash injuries from minor accidents. This can involve:

- **Claiming More Severe Symptoms Than Experienced**: For example, claiming chronic pain, severe headaches, or debilitating dizziness from a low-impact collision. Imagine someone involved in a minor fender bender claiming they now suffer from constant, severe migraines.
- **Fabricating Symptoms**: Inventing symptoms that don't exist to support a claim of severe injury. This is like pretending to have a limp to get sympathy and compensation.
- **Prolonging Recovery**: Claiming a longer recovery period than is medically necessary. For instance, someone might claim they need months of physical therapy for a minor neck strain.

Examples of Exaggerated Whiplash Claims

- **Low-Speed Fender Bender**: A person involved in a low-speed fender bender claims to have suffered severe whiplash resulting in chronic neck pain and disability. They might insist they can no longer work or perform daily activities.
- **Exaggerated Headaches**: An individual exaggerates the frequency and severity of headaches experienced after a minor accident. They might claim they have debilitating headaches every day, preventing them from functioning normally.

- **Costly Medical Treatment**: A claimant claims to have required extensive and costly medical treatment, including surgery, for a relatively minor whiplash injury. They might provide inflated medical bills and reports from unscrupulous medical providers.

Why Exaggerated Claims Occur

Several factors contribute to exaggerated injury claims:

- **Financial Gain**: The primary motivation is often financial, with claimants seeking to maximize compensation. It's like trying to squeeze as much money as possible from the insurance company.
- **Advocate Influence**: In some cases, advocates may encourage clients to exaggerate injuries to increase the value of a claim. They might suggest that a more severe injury will result in a higher payout.
- **Medical Provider Collaboration**: Unscrupulous medical providers may work with claimants to fabricate injuries or unnecessary treatments. They might provide false medical reports or recommend unnecessary procedures to inflate the claim.

The Impact of Exaggerated Claims

Exaggerated injury claims have several negative consequences:

- **Increased Insurance Premiums**: Insurance companies pass the cost of fraudulent claims onto policyholders through higher premiums. It's like everyone having to pay more for a meal because a few people decided to dine and dash.

- **Delayed Legitimate Claims**: Fraudulent claims can lead to increased scrutiny of genuine claims, causing delays in processing legitimate claims. This is like honest customers having to wait longer because the store is busy dealing with shoplifters.
- **Eroded Public Trust**: Exaggerated claims can damage public trust in the insurance industry. People might start to view all claims with suspicion, making it harder for genuine claimants to get the help they need.

Countermeasures

To combat exaggerated injury claims, insurance companies employ various strategies:

- **Thorough Claim Investigations**: Detailed investigations, including medical record reviews and surveillance. This is like a detective piecing together clues to uncover the truth.
- **Expert Medical Reviews**: Consulting independent medical experts to assess the legitimacy of injuries. These experts can provide an unbiased opinion on the severity of the injury.
- **Fraud Detection Units**: Specialized teams dedicated to investigating suspicious claims. These units use various techniques to identify and prevent fraud.
- **Data Analytics**: Using data to identify patterns of fraudulent behavior. Advanced analytics can reveal trends and anomalies that indicate potential fraud.

By understanding the tactics used in exaggerated injury claims and implementing effective countermeasures, insurance companies can better protect themselves and their policyholders from financial loss. This ongoing battle requires vigilance, innovation, and collaboration to ensure a fair and transparent insurance system.

CHAPTER THIRTEEN

Vehicle and Driver Implication in Third-Party Insurance Claims: - Examining the Specific Tactics Used in India

Vehicle and driver implication is a common tactic used by fraudsters to manipulate insurance claims. In the Indian context, this type of fraud is prevalent and often involves complex schemes. Let's break down the common scenarios and challenges, along with examples to illustrate how these fraudulent activities are carried out.

Common Scenarios

1. Non-existent Vehicle

- **Description**: Claiming an accident involving a vehicle that never existed. This involves providing fabricated registration details, fake insurance documents, or even forged vehicle ownership papers.

- **Example**: A claimant might file a claim stating that a high-end car, which is non-existent, was involved in an accident and suffered significant damage. Imagine someone claiming that their luxury sports car was totaled in an accident, but in reality, the car never existed.

2. Stolen Vehicle

- **Description**: A stolen vehicle might be used to stage an accident to claim insurance benefits. The vehicle owner could be completely unaware of the fraudulent activity.
- **Example**: A stolen car is involved in a staged accident. The perpetrators file a claim for damages, while the actual owner remains oblivious to the incident. Picture a thief using a stolen car to stage a crash and then filing a claim as if they were the owner.

3. Vehicle Substitution

- **Description**: A damaged vehicle might be replaced with a more severely damaged one to inflate the claim amount. This often involves collusion between the claimant and a repair shop.
- **Example**: A car with minor scratches is replaced with a car that has been involved in a serious accident to claim higher compensation. Think of someone swapping their lightly scratched car with a wrecked one to get a bigger payout.

4. Driver Impersonation

- **Description**: The individual driving the vehicle at the time of the accident might be different from the person named as the driver in the insurance policy. This is often done to avoid higher premiums or to protect a licensed driver.
- **Example**: An unlicensed driver is involved in an accident, but the claim is filed by a licensed family member to avoid penalties. Imagine a teenager driving without a license, getting into an accident, and then the parent filing the claim as if they were driving.

Challenges in Detection

Detecting vehicle and driver implication fraud can be challenging due to several reasons:

- **Lack of Comprehensive Database**: India lacks a centralized database that can verify vehicle ownership, registration, and insurance details in real-time. This makes it difficult to cross-check information quickly.
- **Collusion**: Fraudsters often work in collusion with other parties, such as repair shops, to create a convincing facade. This network of deceit makes it harder to uncover the truth.
- **Remote Locations**: In rural areas, verifying vehicle and driver details can be time-consuming and resource-intensive due to limited infrastructure. This geographical challenge can be exploited by fraudsters.
- **Forgery Expertise**: Fraudsters often employ sophisticated techniques to forge documents, making it difficult to identify discrepancies. High-quality forgeries can easily deceive even experienced investigators.

Countermeasures

To combat this type of fraud, insurance companies and investigators can implement the following measures:

- **Robust Verification Processes**: Implementing stringent verification procedures for vehicle and driver details, including physical inspection when necessary. This thorough approach can help catch discrepancies early.
- **Data Analytics**: Utilizing data analytics to identify patterns of fraudulent claims based on vehicle and driver information. Advanced analytics can reveal trends and anomalies that indicate potential fraud.
- **Collaboration with Law Enforcement**: Working closely with law enforcement agencies to share information and investigate suspected cases of fraud. This partnership is crucial for gathering evidence and prosecuting fraudsters.
- **Awareness Campaigns**: Educating the public about the consequences of insurance fraud and the importance of providing accurate information. Awareness can deter potential fraudsters and encourage honest behavior.

By combining these efforts, the insurance industry can significantly reduce the impact of vehicle and driver implication fraud, protecting both their financial interests and the integrity of the insurance system.

Claim Exaggeration in Third-Party Insurance – General Overview of Exaggerating Claim Amounts

Claim exaggeration is a prevalent form of insurance fraud where individuals or businesses inflate the extent of damages or injuries to receive a higher compensation amount. This can involve providing false or misleading information, manipulating evidence, or colluding with third parties. Let's explore this issue in more detail, with clear examples to illustrate how these fraudulent activities are carried out.

Common Examples of Claim Exaggeration

1. Exaggerated Injury Claims

- **Inflated Medical Bills**: Claiming treatments or procedures that were not necessary or were less expensive than billed.

- Example: A claimant might visit multiple doctors and undergo unnecessary tests to inflate medical bills. For instance, someone with a minor sprain might claim they needed extensive physical therapy and expensive diagnostic tests.

- **Prolonged Recovery**: Claiming a longer recovery period than medically justified.

  - Example: A person with a minor whiplash injury might claim they need months of rest and rehabilitation, even though they could recover in a few weeks.

- **Fabricated Injuries**: Claiming injuries that did not occur or were less severe than described.

  - Example: A claimant might exaggerate the severity of a whiplash injury, claiming long-term pain and suffering, to justify a higher compensation amount. They might say they have chronic neck pain and migraines, even if they feel fine.

2. Property Damage Exaggeration

- **Inflated Repair Costs**: Providing estimates from fraudulent repair shops or claiming non-existent damages.

  - Example: A claimant might get a repair shop to inflate the cost of fixing a minor dent, claiming it requires extensive bodywork and expensive parts.

- **Overvaluing Possessions**: Claiming higher values for stolen or damaged items.

  - **Example**: Someone might claim that their old, worn-out laptop was a brand-new, high-end model to get a higher payout.

- **Fabricating Losses**: Claiming items that were never owned or were not damaged in the incident.

  - **Example**: A claimant might claim that a completely destroyed car was in excellent condition before the accident to inflate its value. They might provide fake photos or documents to support their claim.

3. Business Interruption Loss Exaggeration

- **Inflated Revenue Loss**: Overstating the financial impact of a business interruption.

  - **Example**: A business owner might exaggerate the loss of revenue following a fire, claiming a significant decline in sales without providing sufficient supporting documentation. They might say their sales dropped by 50% when it was only 10%.

- **Fabricated Expenses**: Claiming additional expenses that were not incurred due to the incident.

  - **Example**: A business might claim they had to hire extra staff or rent additional space to continue operations, even if they didn't.

Techniques Used by Fraudsters

- **Providing False or Misleading Information**: Claimants may provide inaccurate details about the incident, injuries, or damages.

    ◦ **Example**: A person might lie about the speed of the vehicles involved in an accident to make the collision seem more severe.

- **Manipulating Evidence**: Altering or fabricating documents, photographs, or other evidence to support exaggerated claims.

    ◦ **Example**: A claimant might photoshop images of their damaged property to make it look worse than it is.

- **Colluding with Third Parties**: Working with repair shops, medical providers, or other individuals to inflate claim amounts.

    ◦ **Example**: A repair shop might provide inflated estimates, or a doctor might write exaggerated medical reports in exchange for a share of the payout.

- **Exploiting Loopholes**: Taking advantage of ambiguities or gaps in insurance policies to maximize payouts.

- ◦ **Example**: A claimant might find a vague clause in their policy that they can exploit to justify a higher claim.

Challenges in Detecting Claim Exaggeration

- **Subjectivity of Claims**: Assessing the extent of injuries or damages can be subjective, making it difficult to determine if a claim is exaggerated.

  - ◦ **Example**: Pain and suffering are subjective experiences, and it's hard to prove if someone is exaggerating their discomfort.

- **Lack of Evidence**: Fraudsters often carefully plan their schemes, making it challenging to gather sufficient evidence to prove exaggeration.

  - ◦ **Example**: A claimant might destroy or hide evidence that contradicts their exaggerated claims.

- **Complex Insurance Policies**: The intricate details of insurance policies can be exploited by fraudsters to justify inflated claims.

  - ◦ **Example**: A claimant might use complex legal language to argue for a higher payout, knowing that the insurer might not have the resources to contest it.

By understanding the common tactics used by fraudsters and implementing effective fraud prevention measures, insurance companies can mitigate the risks associated with claim exaggeration. This ongoing battle requires vigilance, innovation, and collaboration to ensure a fair and transparent insurance system.

CHAPTER FIFTEEN

Collusion in Insurance Fraud: A Collaborative Approach to Deception - Exploring the Involvement of Multiple Parties in Fraudulent Activities

Collusion in insurance fraud involves the cooperation of multiple parties to create a fraudulent claim. This often includes repair shops, medical professionals, and other individuals who work together to inflate claim amounts or fabricate damages. Let's explore this issue in more detail, with clear examples to illustrate how these fraudulent activities are carried out.

Common Examples of Collusion

1. Repair Shop Collusion

- **Inflated Repair Estimates**: Repair shops provide exaggerated estimates for damages, often including unnecessary repairs or replacement parts.

  - **Example**: A repair shop might claim to have replaced an entire engine when only minor repairs were needed. For instance, a car with a minor oil leak might be billed for a complete engine overhaul.

- **Phantom Parts**: Charging for parts that were never used or replaced.

  - **Example**: A repair shop might bill for a new transmission when the original one was never touched. The invoice might list expensive parts that were never actually installed.

- **Ghost Labor**: Billing for labor that was never performed.

  - **Example**: A repair shop might charge for 20 hours of labor when only 5 hours were actually spent on the repairs. The shop might list multiple technicians working on the car when only one did.

2. Medical Professional Collusion

- **Unnecessary Treatments**: Medical professionals recommend or perform unnecessary treatments or procedures to inflate medical bills.

  - **Example**: A doctor might prescribe a series of expensive physical therapy sessions for a minor sprain that could heal with rest. The patient might be sent for multiple MRIs and X-rays that aren't needed.

- **False Diagnoses**: Providing false diagnoses to justify additional treatments or a longer recovery period.

  - **Example**: A medical professional might diagnose a claimant with a more severe injury than actually suffered to justify extended treatment and higher medical bills. For instance, diagnosing a simple bruise as a fracture.

- **Falsified Medical Records**: Creating or altering medical records to support exaggerated claims.

  - **Example**: A doctor might alter medical records to show that a patient has been receiving treatment for months when they only visited once. The records might list symptoms and treatments that never occurred.

3. Claim Adjuster Collusion

- **Inflated Claim Valuations**: Claim adjusters might deliberately overvalue damages or injuries to benefit claimants or themselves.

  - **Example**: A claim adjuster might approve a repair estimate that is significantly higher than the actual cost of repairs, sharing the excess with the repair shop. The adjuster might list damages that don't exist to increase the payout.

- **Kickbacks**: Claim adjusters may receive kickbacks from repair shops or medical providers for referring clients.

  - **Example**: An adjuster might receive a percentage of the inflated repair costs from the shop in exchange for approving the exaggerated claim. The adjuster might steer claimants to specific shops or doctors who participate in the scheme.

4. Advocate Collusion

- **Encouraging Fraudulent Claims**: Advocates might advise clients to exaggerate injuries or damages to increase the potential settlement.

  - **Example**: An advocate might suggest that a claimant claim a more severe whiplash injury to increase the chances of a higher settlement. They might coach the claimant on what symptoms to report.

- **Sharing Fees**: Advocates may agree to share a portion of the settlement with claimants or other parties involved in the fraud.

  - **Example**: An advocate might agree to split the settlement with the claimant or other involved parties, incentivizing everyone to exaggerate the claim. They might also share fees with doctors or repair shops involved in the scheme.

Challenges in Detecting Collusion

- **Complex Relationships**: Identifying and proving collusion can be challenging due to the complex relationships between involved parties.

  - **Example**: A repair shop, doctor, and claim adjuster might all be in on the scheme, making it difficult to trace the connections and prove collusion.

- **Lack of Evidence**: Fraudsters often take steps to conceal their involvement, making it difficult to gather evidence.

  - **Example**: They might use fake invoices, altered medical records, and other forged documents to cover their tracks.

- **Insider Knowledge**: Individuals with inside knowledge of the insurance industry can exploit vulnerabilities in the system.

  - **Example**: A claim adjuster might know exactly how to manipulate the system to avoid detection, using their expertise to orchestrate the fraud.

Countermeasures

To combat collusion, insurance companies can implement the following measures:

- **Thorough Investigations**: Conducting detailed investigations into repair shops, medical providers, and other involved parties.

- **Example**: Investigators might visit repair shops to verify the work done, interview medical professionals, and cross-check documents to uncover discrepancies.

- **Data Analytics**: Using data analytics to identify patterns of suspicious claims and potential collusion.

  - **Example**: Advanced analytics can reveal unusual patterns, such as frequent high-value claims from the same repair shop or doctor, indicating possible collusion.

- **Audits and Inspections**: Regularly auditing repair shops and medical providers to detect fraudulent activities.

  - **Example**: Routine audits can uncover inflated repair costs, unnecessary treatments, and other signs of fraud.

- **Employee Training**: Educating employees about the signs of collusion and how to report suspicious behavior.

  - **Example**: Training sessions can help employees recognize red flags, such as unusually high estimates or frequent referrals to the same providers.

- **Collaboration with Law Enforcement**: Working with law enforcement agencies to investigate and prosecute cases of collusion.

- ○ **Example**: Joint investigations with law enforcement can provide the resources and authority needed to gather evidence and bring fraudsters to justice.

By implementing these measures, insurance companies can reduce the risk of collusion and protect their financial interests. This collaborative approach to combating fraud ensures a fair and transparent insurance system for all policyholders.

Insurance investigators play a crucial role in uncovering fraudulent schemes and protecting the integrity of the insurance industry. Their work involves a combination of investigative techniques, analytical skills, and collaboration with various stakeholders. Here's a closer look at their role:

CHAPTER SIXTEEN

Behind the scenes -Key Responsibilities of Insurance Investigators

1. Conducting Thorough Investigations

- **Site Visits and Inspections**: Investigators visit the scene of accidents or incidents to gather evidence, take photographs, and interview witnesses. For example, in the case of a staged accident, they might inspect the damage to determine if it aligns with the reported events.

- **Reviewing Documentation**: They meticulously review all relevant documents, such as medical records, repair bills, and police reports, to identify inconsistencies or signs of fraud. For instance, they might compare medical bills to standard treatment costs to spot inflated charges.

2. Analyzing Data

- **Pattern Recognition**: Investigators use data analytics to identify patterns and anomalies in claims. This can help detect suspicious activities, such as multiple claims from the same individual or repair shop. For example, if a particular repair shop consistently submits high-cost estimates, it might warrant further investigation.
- **Cross-Referencing Information**: They cross-reference information from various sources, such as vehicle registration databases and insurance records, to verify the accuracy of claims. This helps in identifying non-existent vehicles or false ownership claims.

3. Interviewing and Surveillance

- **Interviewing Claimants and Witnesses**: Investigators conduct interviews to gather detailed accounts of the incident. They look for discrepancies in the stories provided by different parties. For example, if a claimant's account of an accident differs significantly from witness statements, it raises red flags.
- **Surveillance**: In cases of suspected exaggerated injury claims, investigators might conduct surveillance to observe the claimant's activities. For instance, if someone claiming severe back pain is seen engaging in physical activities, it contradicts their claim.

4. Collaborating with Experts

- **Medical Experts**: Investigators often consult with independent medical experts to assess the legitimacy of injury claims. These experts can provide unbiased opinions on the severity and cause of injuries.

- **Automotive Experts**: In cases involving vehicle damage, they work with automotive experts to evaluate the extent of damage and the necessity of repairs. This helps in detecting inflated repair costs or unnecessary repairs.

5. Working with Law Enforcement

- **Sharing Information**: Investigators collaborate with law enforcement agencies to share information and resources. This partnership is essential for gathering evidence and prosecuting fraudsters.
- **Joint Investigations**: In complex cases, they might conduct joint investigations with law enforcement to uncover organized fraud rings. For example, a network of individuals staging accidents might require coordinated efforts to dismantle.

Examples of Investigative Techniques

- **Forensic Analysis**: Using forensic techniques to analyze physical evidence, such as vehicle damage or medical records, to uncover signs of tampering or fabrication.
- **Digital Investigations**: Examining digital footprints, such as social media activity, to gather evidence. For instance, a claimant posting about a vacation while claiming to be bedridden raises suspicion.
- **Undercover Operations**: In some cases, investigators might go undercover to gather information about fraudulent activities. This could involve posing as a customer at a repair shop suspected of inflating repair costs.

Impact of Insurance Investigators

- **Reducing Fraudulent Claims**: By uncovering fraudulent schemes, investigators help reduce the number of fraudulent claims, which in turn helps keep insurance premiums lower for honest policyholders.
- **Deterring Future Fraud**: The presence of skilled investigators acts as a deterrent to potential fraudsters, knowing that their schemes are likely to be uncovered.
- **Protecting Company Finances**: By preventing fraudulent payouts, investigators protect the financial health of insurance companies, ensuring they can continue to provide coverage to genuine claimants.

Insurance investigators are the frontline defense against fraud, using a combination of investigative prowess, analytical skills, and collaboration to uncover and prevent fraudulent schemes. Their work is essential in maintaining the integrity and trustworthiness of the insurance industry.

The Intricate World of Insurance Investigations – An Overview of the Investigation Process

Insurance investigations form a critical component of the risk management strategy for insurance companies. These investigations delve into the circumstances surrounding insurance claims to verify the legitimacy of the claim, assess the extent of loss, and detect potential fraud. Let's explore the scope, roles, challenges, and future of insurance investigations in more detail.

The Scope of Insurance Investigations

Insurance investigations encompass a wide range of claims, including:

- **Property Insurance:** Investigating claims related to fires, floods, theft, and other property-related losses.

- ◦ **Example**: After a house fire, an investigator might examine the scene, interview witnesses, and review fire department reports to determine the cause and extent of the damage.

- **Liability Insurance**: Handling claims arising from accidents, injuries, or property damage caused by the insured.

  - ◦ **Example**: In a slip-and-fall case at a store, the investigator might review surveillance footage, interview witnesses, and inspect the site to verify the claim.

- **Life Insurance**: Investigating death claims, policy fraud, and beneficiary disputes.

  - ◦ **Example**: If a life insurance claim seems suspicious, the investigator might verify the death certificate, interview family members, and check for any signs of foul play.

- **Health Insurance**: Examining medical claims, fraudulent billing, and policy compliance.

  - ◦ **Example**: An investigator might review medical records and billing statements to ensure that the treatments claimed were necessary and actually provided.

- **Commercial Insurance**: Investigating business interruption, equipment breakdown, and liability claims.

- **Example**: After a factory fire, the investigator might assess the damage to equipment, verify business interruption losses, and ensure that the claim aligns with the policy terms.

The Role of the Insurance Investigator

An insurance investigator is tasked with several key responsibilities:

- **Claim Verification**: Gathering evidence to substantiate the claim, including witness statements, photographs, and documentation.

  - **Example**: In a car accident claim, the investigator might take photos of the damage, interview the drivers and witnesses, and review police reports.

- **Fraud Detection**: Identifying patterns of suspicious activity or fraudulent claims.

  - **Example**: If a claimant has a history of frequent and similar claims, the investigator might look deeper into the current claim for signs of fraud.

- **Loss Assessment**: Determining the extent of the loss and calculating the appropriate compensation.

  - **Example**: After a burglary, the investigator might inventory the stolen items, assess their value, and determine the rightful compensation.

- **Policy Interpretation**: Ensuring that the claim falls within the scope of the insurance policy.

- ○ **Example**: The investigator might review the policy terms to confirm that the claimed loss is covered and that all conditions are met.

- **Liaison with External Parties**: Coordinating with law enforcement, repair shops, medical providers, and other relevant parties.

  - ○ **Example**: In a health insurance fraud case, the investigator might work with doctors to verify the authenticity of medical treatments and bills.

Challenges Faced by Insurance Investigators

Insurance investigators operate in a complex environment with numerous challenges:

- **Fraudulent Claims**: The increasing sophistication of fraudsters requires investigators to stay updated on the latest fraud schemes.

  - ○ **Example**: Fraudsters might use advanced technology to create fake documents or stage accidents, making it harder to detect fraud.

- **Time Constraints**: Insurance claims often have strict deadlines, putting pressure on investigators to complete their work efficiently.

  - ○ **Example**: An investigator might have only a few days to gather all necessary evidence and submit a report.

- **Resource Constraints**: Limited manpower and financial resources can hinder the investigation process.

- **Example**: An investigator might have to handle multiple cases simultaneously, affecting the thoroughness of each investigation.

- **Legal and Regulatory Compliance**: Navigating complex legal and regulatory frameworks can be time-consuming.

  - **Example**: Investigators must ensure that their methods comply with privacy laws and other regulations.

- **Customer Relations**: Balancing the need to protect the insurer's interests with maintaining positive relationships with policyholders.

  - **Example**: Investigators must handle claims sensitively to avoid alienating honest policyholders while still being thorough.

The Future of Insurance Investigations

The insurance industry is undergoing rapid transformation, driven by technological advancements and changing customer expectations. This is also impacting the role of insurance investigators:

- **Advancements in Technology**: The use of drones, artificial intelligence, and data analytics is enhancing investigative capabilities.

  - **Example**: Drones can be used to survey large disaster areas quickly, while AI can analyze vast amounts of data to detect fraud patterns.

- **Focus on Prevention**: Proactive measures to prevent fraud, such as risk assessment and fraud detection systems, are becoming increasingly important.

  - ◦ **Example**: Predictive analytics can identify high-risk claims before they are paid out, allowing for early intervention.

- **Customer Experience**: Investigators must balance the need for thorough investigations with providing excellent customer service.

  - ◦ **Example**: Streamlining the investigation process and keeping claimants informed can improve customer satisfaction.

- **Remote Investigations**: The increasing use of technology enables remote investigations, expanding the reach of investigators.

  - ◦ **Example**: Virtual inspections and remote interviews can be conducted using video conferencing tools, making it easier to investigate claims in remote areas.

By addressing the challenges and leveraging emerging technologies, insurance investigators can play a crucial role in protecting the financial interests of insurance companies and maintaining the integrity of the insurance industry. Their work ensures that genuine claims are honored while fraudulent activities are detected and prevented.

CHAPTER EIGHTEEN

The Role of the Insurance Investigator – Detailing the Responsibilities of an Investigator

An insurance investigator is a crucial cog in the machinery of the insurance industry. Their role extends beyond simply processing claims; it involves a meticulous examination of every aspect of a claim to ensure its legitimacy. Let's break down their core responsibilities with clear examples to illustrate their importance.

Core Responsibilities

1. Claim Verification

- **Description**: This is the fundamental role of an investigator. They must meticulously examine all supporting documents, including medical reports, repair bills, police reports, and witness statements, to verify their authenticity and consistency.

- **Example**: In a car accident case, an investigator might cross-verify the repair estimate with standard market rates or inspect the damaged vehicle to assess the extent of damage claimed. If a claimant says their car needs a new engine, the investigator might check if the damage really warrants such a costly repair.

2. Fraud Detection

- **Description**: Insurance investigators are the first line of defense against fraud. They employ various techniques like data analysis, surveillance, and interviews to identify patterns of suspicious activity.
- **Example**: An investigator might notice a cluster of similar claims from a particular geographic area, indicating a potential fraud ring. For instance, if multiple claims from the same neighborhood all involve similar types of damage, it might suggest coordinated fraud.

3. Loss Assessment

- **Description**: Determining the actual loss incurred is crucial for accurate claim settlement. Investigators must assess the extent of damage, evaluate the value of lost property, and estimate the cost of repairs or replacements.
- **Example**: In a fire loss, an investigator would assess the damage to the property, its contents, and any potential business interruption losses. They might calculate the cost to rebuild the structure, replace damaged goods, and compensate for lost business income.

4. Policy Interpretation

- **Description**: A deep understanding of insurance policies is essential. Investigators must ensure that the claim falls within the policy's coverage and that there are no exclusions or limitations applicable.
- **Example**: In a homeowner's insurance claim, an investigator must determine if the policy covers flood damage, as it's often excluded in standard policies. They might review the policy terms to see if the damage from a recent flood is covered or excluded.

5. Liaison with External Parties

- **Description**: Insurance investigators often interact with various external parties like law enforcement, repair shops, medical providers, and claimants. Effective communication and relationship building are crucial for gathering information and building a strong case.
- **Example**: An investigator might liaise with a police officer to obtain an accident report or with a medical expert to assess the validity of injury claims. They might also work with repair shops to verify the cost and necessity of repairs.

In Essence

Insurance investigators are the detectives of the insurance world, working diligently to protect the insurer's interests while ensuring fair treatment for policyholders. Their work is multifaceted and requires a combination of analytical skills, investigative acumen, and interpersonal abilities. They play a vital role in maintaining the integrity of the insurance industry by ensuring that claims are legitimate and accurately assessed.

Claim Verification: The Cornerstone of Insurance - The Process of Verifying the Authenticity of Claims

Claim verification is the bedrock of the insurance industry. It's a meticulous process that ensures the legitimacy of a claim and prevents fraudulent activities. Think of it as the foundation of a house; without a solid foundation, the entire structure is at risk.

The Verification Process

Claim verification involves a systematic examination of all supporting documentation provided by the policyholder. This includes:

- **Documentation Review**: Verifying the authenticity and consistency of documents such as police reports, medical bills, repair estimates, photographs, and witness statements.

  ○ **Example**: If a claimant submits a repair bill for a car accident, the investigator might compare it with standard market rates to ensure the costs are reasonable. It's like checking the price of a product online to make sure you're not being overcharged.

- **Data Analysis**: Cross-referencing information from various sources to identify discrepancies or anomalies. This might involve checking the claimant's history, comparing repair estimates with industry standards, or analyzing accident reports for inconsistencies.

  ○ **Example**: If a claimant has a history of multiple similar claims, it might raise a red flag. It's similar to noticing a pattern of repeated absences in an employee's attendance record.

- **On-Site Inspections**: In many cases, physical inspection of the damaged property or vehicle is necessary to assess the extent of loss and verify the accuracy of the claim.

  ○ **Example**: An investigator might visit the site of a house fire to assess the damage firsthand. This is akin to a detective visiting a crime scene to gather evidence.

- **Interviewing Claimants and Witnesses**: Gathering firsthand information by interviewing the policyholder, witnesses, and other involved parties.

  - **Example**: In a slip-and-fall claim, the investigator might interview store employees and customers who witnessed the incident. It's like a journalist conducting interviews to get multiple perspectives on a story.

- **Expert Assessments**: Consulting with experts, such as engineers, doctors, or appraisers, to evaluate the validity of claims.

  - **Example**: For a complex machinery breakdown claim, an engineer might be consulted to determine if the damage was due to wear and tear or a sudden accident. This is similar to getting a second opinion from a specialist doctor.

Key Areas of Focus

- **Identity Verification**: Ensuring that the claimant is the rightful policyholder and has the authority to file the claim.

  - **Example**: Verifying the claimant's identity is like checking a passport at the airport to ensure the traveler is who they say they are.

- **Policy Coverage**: Confirming that the loss is covered under the terms and conditions of the insurance policy.

- ○ **Example**: If a homeowner claims flood damage, the investigator must check if the policy includes flood coverage. It's like reading the fine print of a contract to understand what is included.

- **Loss Assessment**: Determining the actual loss incurred and calculating the appropriate compensation.

  - ○ **Example**: After a burglary, the investigator might inventory the stolen items and assess their value. This is similar to an appraiser determining the value of a piece of art.

- **Fraud Detection**: Identifying any signs of fraudulent activity, such as inflated claims, staged accidents, or forged documents.

  - ○ **Example**: If a claimant submits a bill for a luxury item that wasn't listed in the original inventory, it might indicate fraud. It's like spotting a counterfeit bill in a stack of genuine currency.

Challenges in Claim Verification

- **Fraudulent Documents**: Fraudsters often employ sophisticated techniques to create fake or altered documents.

  - ○ **Example**: A claimant might submit a doctored medical bill to inflate the claim amount. Detecting such fraud is like identifying a fake painting among genuine masterpieces.

- **Complex Claims**: Large-scale losses, such as those caused by natural disasters, can present significant verification challenges due to the volume of claims.

    ◦ **Example**: After a major flood, an investigator might have to verify hundreds of claims, each with its own complexities. It's like sorting through a mountain of paperwork to find the important documents.

- **Time Constraints**: Insurance companies often operate under tight deadlines, putting pressure on investigators to complete their work efficiently.

    ◦ **Example**: An investigator might have only a few days to gather all necessary evidence and submit a report. It's like a student cramming for an exam with a looming deadline.

- **Customer Satisfaction**: Balancing the need for thorough verification with maintaining positive customer relationships can be challenging.

    ◦ **Example**: Investigators must handle claims sensitively to avoid alienating honest policyholders while still being thorough. It's like a doctor delivering a difficult diagnosis with empathy and care.

By conducting thorough claim verification, insurance companies can protect themselves against fraudulent activities, ensure accurate claim settlements, and maintain the trust of their policyholders. This meticulous process is essential for the integrity and sustainability of the insurance industry.

CHAPTER TWENTY

Fraud Detection in Insurance Claims – Techniques and Challenges in Identifying Fraudulent Claims

Fraud detection is a critical component of the insurance investigation process. It involves identifying patterns, inconsistencies, and anomalies in claims data that may indicate fraudulent activity. Think of it as a detective piecing together clues to solve a mystery.

Common Fraud Indicators

1. Pattern Recognition

- **Description**: Identifying unusual claim patterns, such as multiple claims from the same address, similar accident descriptions, or claims with identical repair costs.

- **Example**: If several claims come from the same address within a short period, it might indicate a fraud ring. It's like noticing that multiple thefts in a neighborhood all happen at the same house.

2. Exaggerated Losses

- **Description**: Claims with unusually high damage estimates or inflated valuations compared to industry standards.
- **Example**: A claimant might report that their old car, worth $5,000, was totaled and claim $20,000 in damages. It's like someone trying to sell a used item at the price of a brand-new one.

3. Inconsistent Information

- **Description**: Discrepancies in witness statements, police reports, or medical records.
- **Example**: If a witness says the accident happened at noon, but the police report states it occurred at midnight, it raises suspicion. It's like two people giving completely different accounts of the same event.

4. Suspicious Documentation

- **Description**: Forged or altered documents, such as repair bills, medical records, or vehicle ownership papers.
- **Example**: A repair bill might show work done on parts that were never damaged. It's like receiving a receipt for groceries you never bought.

5. Claim History

- **Description**: Reviewing the claimant's history for previous claims, excessive claims, or a pattern of suspicious activity.
- **Example**: If a claimant has filed multiple similar claims in a short period, it might indicate fraud. It's like someone repeatedly claiming their phone was stolen to get new ones.

Examples of Fraud Detection
1. Staged Accidents

- **Description**: Detecting patterns of staged accidents by analyzing accident reports, witness statements, and injury claims.
- **Example**: Multiple accidents occurring at the same location with similar injury patterns might indicate a staged event. It's like noticing that every car crash at a particular intersection involves the same type of injury.

2. Inflated Repair Costs

- **Description**: Identifying repair shops with consistently high repair estimates or those that frequently work with specific claimants.
- **Example**: A repair shop might always charge double the standard rate for repairs. It's like a restaurant consistently overcharging for meals compared to others in the area.

3. Phantom Claims

- **Description**: Detecting claims for non-existent property or injuries by cross-referencing information with public databases or insurance records.
- **Example**: A claimant might report a stolen car that they never owned. It's like someone claiming their imaginary friend was kidnapped.

4. Organized Fraud Rings

- **Description**: Recognizing patterns of collusion between multiple individuals or businesses to defraud insurance companies.
- **Example**: A group of people might work together to stage accidents and file multiple claims. It's like a team of con artists running a scam together.

Advanced Fraud Detection Techniques
1. Data Analytics

- **Description**: Utilizing data mining and machine learning to identify complex fraud patterns and anomalies.
- **Example**: Algorithms can analyze vast amounts of data to spot unusual patterns, such as a sudden spike in claims from a specific area. It's like using a magnifying glass to find tiny clues in a large puzzle.

2. Social Media Analysis

- **Description**: Examining social media profiles for inconsistencies or evidence of fraudulent activity.
- **Example**: A claimant might post photos of a vacation while claiming to be bedridden due to an injury. It's like

catching someone in a lie by checking their public diary.

3. Geographic Profiling

- **Description**: Analyzing claim locations to identify clusters of suspicious claims.
- **Example**: If many claims come from a small geographic area, it might indicate a local fraud ring. It's like noticing that all the burglaries in a city happen in the same neighborhood.

4. Network Analysis

- **Description**: Identifying relationships between claimants, repair shops, and other parties involved in fraudulent schemes.
- **Example**: If the same repair shop is linked to multiple suspicious claims, it might be part of a fraud network. It's like connecting the dots in a conspiracy theory to see the bigger picture.

By employing these techniques and maintaining a vigilant approach, insurance companies can significantly reduce the impact of fraud and protect their financial interests. Detecting fraud is like solving a complex puzzle, requiring keen observation, analytical skills, and sometimes a bit of intuition.

CHAPTER TWENTY-ONE

Loss Assessment: Determining the Extent of Loss – Evaluating the Financial Impact of a Loss

Loss assessment is a critical phase in the insurance claims process. It involves accurately determining the financial value of the loss incurred by the insured. Think of it as a detective piecing together clues to understand the full picture of a crime scene. This process requires a meticulous evaluation of the damaged property, considering factors such as depreciation, market value, and repair costs.

Key Components of Loss Assessment

1. Property Valuation

- **Description**: Determining the fair market value of the damaged or lost property at the time of the loss. This involves considering factors such as age, condition, and comparable market prices.

- **Example**: If a house is damaged in a fire, the investigator will assess its current market value by comparing it to similar houses in the area. It's like appraising a piece of art by looking at similar works sold recently.

2. Damage Assessment

- **Description**: Evaluating the extent of damage to the property and determining the cost of repairs or replacement. This may involve consulting with experts like engineers, contractors, or appraisers.
- **Example**: After a car accident, an investigator might consult a mechanic to estimate the repair costs. It's similar to a doctor diagnosing an illness and prescribing the necessary treatment.

3. Depreciation

- **Description**: Accounting for the depreciation of property over time. Depreciation reduces the value of the property and, consequently, the insurance claim amount.
- **Example**: A five-year-old laptop will be worth less than a brand-new one, even if it was in perfect condition before the loss. It's like the value of a car decreasing the moment you drive it off the lot.

4. Salvage Value

- **Description**: Determining the value of any recoverable items or materials from the damaged property. This amount is typically deducted from the overall claim.

- **Example**: If a car is totaled, but the engine is still in good condition, the value of the engine will be deducted from the claim. It's like selling parts of a broken appliance to recoup some of the cost.

5. Additional Costs

- **Description**: Considering expenses incurred as a result of the loss, such as temporary housing, storage, or rental car fees.
- **Example**: If a family's home is uninhabitable after a fire, the cost of staying in a hotel will be included in the claim. It's like adding up all the extra costs you incur when your main resource is unavailable.

Challenges in Loss Assessment
1. Determining Fair Market Value

- **Description**: Accurately assessing the value of damaged or lost property can be complex, especially for unique or antique items.
- **Example**: Valuing a rare painting damaged in a flood requires expertise and comparison with similar rare items. It's like trying to price a one-of-a-kind collectible.

2. Estimating Repair Costs

- **Description**: Obtaining accurate repair estimates can be challenging, as repair costs can vary depending on factors such as labor rates, material costs, and availability.
- **Example**: The cost to repair a roof might vary significantly between contractors. It's like getting

different quotes for fixing a leaky faucet.

3. Depreciation Calculation

- **Description**: Determining the appropriate depreciation rate for different types of property can be complex.
- **Example**: Calculating how much a ten-year-old car has depreciated involves considering its make, model, and condition. It's like figuring out how much wear and tear has reduced the value of a used book.

4. Fraudulent Claims

- **Description**: Inflated values or false claims can complicate the loss assessment process.
- **Example**: A claimant might exaggerate the value of stolen jewelry to get a higher payout. It's like someone inflating the price of a used item they're selling online.

Role of Technology in Loss Assessment

Technology has significantly improved the accuracy and efficiency of loss assessment. Tools such as:

- **Property Valuation Databases**: Provide comparable market data for property valuation.

  - **Example**: Using a database to find recent sales of similar houses helps determine the value of a damaged home. It's like checking online listings to price your house for sale.

- **Estimating Software**: Assist in calculating repair costs and depreciation.

- ○ **Example**: Software can quickly generate repair estimates based on current labor and material costs. It's like using a budgeting app to track your expenses.

- **Drone Technology**: Can be used to assess property damage from aerial perspectives.

  - ○ **Example**: Drones can survey large areas of damage after a natural disaster, providing detailed images for assessment. It's like using a bird's-eye view to get a complete picture of a landscape.

By employing advanced technologies and experienced professionals, insurance companies can conduct thorough and accurate loss assessments, ensuring fair compensation for policyholders. This meticulous process is essential for maintaining trust and integrity in the insurance industry.

CHAPTER TWENTY-TWO

The Verification Process: Ensuring Claim Legitimacy - A Deeper Look into the Verification Process

Claim verification is the cornerstone of accurate and fair insurance settlements. It involves a meticulous examination of all aspects of a claim to validate its legitimacy and prevent fraudulent activities. Think of it as a detective piecing together clues to solve a mystery.

Key Steps in the Verification Process

1. Documentation Review

- **Description**: This is the initial step where all supporting documents provided by the claimant are scrutinized.
- **Components:**

- ○ **Police Reports**: Verifying the details of the incident, date, time, and involved parties.

  - ▪ **Example**: If a car accident claim is filed, the investigator checks the police report to confirm the accident details. It's like reading a witness statement to understand what happened.

- ○ **Medical Reports**: Assessing the nature of injuries, treatment provided, and medical expenses.

  - ▪ **Example**: For an injury claim, the investigator reviews medical records to ensure the treatments match the injuries reported. It's like a doctor reviewing a patient's medical history.

- ○ **Repair Estimates**: Comparing the estimated repair costs with industry standards and the extent of damage.

  - ▪ **Example**: If a house is damaged in a storm, the investigator compares repair estimates with typical costs for similar repairs. It's like getting multiple quotes before choosing a contractor.

- ○ **Photographs**: Verifying the scene of the accident or damage to the property.

  - ▪ **Example**: Photos of a damaged vehicle help the investigator assess the extent of damage. It's like using photos to document evidence at a crime scene.

- ○ **Witness Statements**: Corroborating the claimant's version of events.

  - ▪ **Example**: Witnesses to a car accident provide statements that the investigator uses to verify the claimant's account. It's like cross-examining witnesses in a court case.

2. Data Analysis

- **Description**: Insurance companies employ sophisticated data analytics tools to cross-reference information from various sources.
- **Components**:

  - ○ **Claim History Analysis**: Checking for previous claims by the same claimant or from the same address.

    - ▪ **Example**: If a claimant has filed multiple similar claims, it might indicate a pattern of fraud. It's like noticing repeated absences in an employee's attendance record.

  - ○ **Repair Shop Analysis**: Evaluating the reputation and claim history of involved repair shops.

    - ▪ **Example**: A repair shop with a history of inflated estimates might be flagged for further investigation. It's like checking reviews before choosing a service provider.

- **Geographic Analysis**: Identifying patterns of fraudulent claims in specific areas.

  - **Example**: A spike in claims from a particular neighborhood might indicate a local fraud ring. It's like mapping crime hotspots in a city.

3. On-Site Inspections

- **Description**: In many cases, a physical inspection of the damaged property or vehicle is crucial.
- **Components**:

  - **Assessing the Extent of Damage**: Determining if the claimed damages match the actual condition.

    - **Example**: Inspecting a damaged roof to see if the reported damage matches the actual condition. It's like a mechanic checking a car for issues.

  - **Verifying the Existence of Damaged Property**: Ensuring that the claimed items were indeed owned by the claimant.

    - **Example**: Confirming that a stolen item was actually owned by the claimant. It's like verifying ownership of a lost pet.

  - **Identifying Potential Salvage Value**: Evaluating if any salvageable parts can be recovered.

    - **Example**: Assessing if parts of a totaled car can be sold for salvage. It's like recycling parts of a broken appliance.

4. Interviewing Claimants and Witnesses

- **Description**: Gathering firsthand information from the claimant and witnesses is essential to corroborate the claim.
- **Components**:

  - **Asking Probing Questions**: Uncovering inconsistencies or discrepancies.

    - **Example**: Asking detailed questions about the accident to spot any inconsistencies. It's like a journalist digging deeper into a story.

  - **Verifying Credibility**: Ensuring the information provided is credible.

    - **Example**: Cross-checking witness statements with other evidence. It's like fact-checking a news article.

  - **Building Rapport**: Encouraging honest communication.

    - **Example**: Establishing trust with the claimant to get accurate information. It's like a therapist building rapport with a patient.

5. Expert Assessments

- **Description**: In complex cases, involving experts like engineers, doctors, or appraisers is necessary.
- **Components**:

  - **Determining the Cause of Damage or Injury**: Using expert knowledge to understand the cause.

    - **Example**: An engineer might determine if a building collapse was due to structural issues. It's like a forensic scientist analyzing evidence.

  - **Assessing the Extent of Loss**: Evaluating the financial impact.

    - **Example**: An appraiser might assess the value of damaged artwork. It's like an art critic evaluating a painting.

  - **Providing an Unbiased Opinion**: Offering an objective assessment.

    - **Example**: A doctor providing an independent medical evaluation. It's like a judge giving an impartial verdict.

Example: Vehicle Accident Claim

In a car accident claim, the verification process might involve:

- **Reviewing the Police Report**: Checking details about the accident, involved vehicles, and injuries.

- **Example**: Confirming the accident's time and location. It's like verifying an alibi in a criminal investigation.

- **Comparing Repair Estimates**: Identifying discrepancies between different repair shops.

  - **Example**: Noticing one shop's estimate is significantly higher than others. It's like comparing prices at different stores.

- **Inspecting the Damaged Vehicle**: Assessing the extent of damage and verifying the claimed repairs.

  - **Example**: Checking if the reported damage matches the actual condition. It's like a home inspector evaluating a property's condition.

- **Interviewing the Claimant and Witnesses**: Gathering firsthand accounts of the accident.

  - **Example**: Asking witnesses to describe what they saw. It's like interviewing eyewitnesses to a crime.

- **Consulting with a Vehicle Valuation Expert**: Determining the vehicle's pre-accident value.

  - **Example**: An expert assessing the car's market value before the accident. It's like an appraiser valuing a piece of real estate.

By following these steps and employing advanced technologies, insurance companies can effectively verify the legitimacy of claims, detect fraudulent activities, and ensure fair compensation for policyholders. This thorough process is essential for maintaining trust and integrity in the insurance industry.

CHAPTER TWENTY-THREE

Challenges in Claim Verification - Obstacles Faced by Investigators During Verification

The process of claim verification is fraught with challenges that demand meticulous attention and expertise. Let's explore these challenges with examples and similes to make them more relatable.

Challenges in Document Verification

1. Forged Documents

- **Description**: Fraudsters often employ sophisticated techniques to create fake or altered documents. Identifying these forgeries requires specialized skills and tools.

- **Example**: A claimant might submit a doctored medical bill to inflate the claim amount. Detecting such fraud is like identifying a counterfeit bill among genuine currency.

- **Simile**: It's like trying to spot a fake painting in a gallery full of masterpieces.

2. Inconsistent Information

- **Description**: Discrepancies between different documents or within the same document can hinder the verification process and raise suspicion of fraud.
- **Example**: If the police report states the accident happened at noon, but the medical report says the injuries were treated at midnight, it raises red flags.
- **Simile**: It's like reading a story where the details don't match up, making you question the truth.

3. Missing Documentation

- **Description**: Incomplete documentation can make it difficult to assess the legitimacy of a claim and may necessitate additional investigations.
- **Example**: A claimant might not provide all the necessary receipts for repairs, making it hard to verify the expenses.
- **Simile**: It's like trying to complete a puzzle with missing pieces.

Challenges in On-Site Inspections
1. Remote Locations

- **Description**: In rural areas, accessing accident sites or damaged property can be time-consuming and resource-intensive.
- **Example**: An investigator might need to travel several hours to inspect a damaged farmhouse.

- **Simile**: It's like embarking on a long journey to find a hidden treasure.

2. Weather Conditions

- **Description**: Adverse weather can impede on-site inspections and delay the claims process.
- **Example**: Heavy rain might make it impossible to inspect a flood-damaged property.
- **Simile**: It's like trying to paint a picture in the middle of a storm.

3. Safety Concerns

- **Description**: Inspecting accident sites or damaged property can pose safety risks to investigators.
- **Example**: Entering a partially collapsed building to assess damage can be dangerous.
- **Simile**: It's like walking through a minefield, where every step must be taken with caution.

Challenges in Interviewing Claimants and Witnesses
1. Language Barriers

- **Description**: Communicating with claimants and witnesses who speak different languages can be challenging and may require interpreters.
- **Example**: An investigator might need an interpreter to interview a non-English-speaking witness.
- **Simile**: It's like trying to solve a mystery with clues written in a foreign language.

2. Reluctant Witnesses

- **Description**: Some witnesses may be hesitant to provide information or may have conflicting interests.
- **Example**: A witness might be unwilling to testify against a neighbor involved in a fraudulent claim.
- **Simile**: It's like pulling teeth to get someone to speak up.

3. Memory Lapses

- **Description**: The passage of time can affect the accuracy of witness statements, making it difficult to verify information.
- **Example**: A witness might forget key details about an accident that happened months ago.
- **Simile**: It's like trying to recall a dream after waking up.

Challenges in Expert Assessment
1. Availability of Experts

- **Description**: Securing the services of qualified experts in a timely manner can be difficult, especially in specialized areas.
- **Example**: Finding a structural engineer to assess a building collapse might take time.
- **Simile**: It's like searching for a needle in a haystack.

2. Conflicting Expert Opinions

- **Description**: Different experts may provide conflicting assessments, making it challenging to reach a definitive conclusion.
- **Example**: One doctor might diagnose a minor injury, while another sees it as severe.

- **Simile**: It's like two chefs arguing over the best recipe for the same dish.

3. Cost of Expert Services

- **Description**: Engaging experts can be expensive, impacting the overall cost of the investigation.
- **Example**: Hiring a forensic accountant to audit financial records can be costly.
- **Simile**: It's like paying a premium for a top-notch detective to solve a case.

Overcoming These Challenges

Overcoming these challenges requires a combination of skilled investigators, advanced technology, and robust processes. By addressing these issues effectively, insurance companies can improve the accuracy of claim assessments and protect their financial interests. It's like assembling a team of superheroes, each with their unique skills, to tackle a complex mission.

Handling conflicting witness statements is a critical part of the investigation process. Investigators must carefully analyze and reconcile these discrepancies to uncover the truth. Here are some steps they typically take, illustrated with examples and similes:

CHAPTER TWENTY-FOUR

Strategies for Handling Inconsistent Witness Statements

1. Detailed Interviews

- **Description**: Conducting thorough and detailed interviews with each witness to gather as much information as possible.
- **Example**: If two witnesses give different accounts of a car accident, the investigator might ask each one to describe the event in detail, including the time, location, and sequence of events.
- **Simile**: It's like a journalist interviewing multiple sources to get a comprehensive story.

2. Cross-Referencing Statements

- **Description**: Comparing the statements of different witnesses to identify common points and discrepancies.
- **Example**: If one witness says the accident happened at noon and another says it was at night, the investigator

will look for other evidence, like traffic camera footage, to determine the correct time.

- **Simile**: It's like a detective cross-checking alibis to find inconsistencies.

3. Corroborating with Physical Evidence

- **Description**: Using physical evidence to support or refute witness statements.
- **Example**: If witnesses disagree on the speed of the vehicles involved in an accident, the investigator might examine skid marks and vehicle damage to estimate the speed.
- **Simile**: It's like a scientist using experiments to test a hypothesis.

4. Assessing Credibility

- **Description**: Evaluating the credibility of each witness based on their background, relationship to the parties involved, and consistency of their statements.
- **Example**: A witness with a history of honesty and no vested interest in the outcome is considered more credible than one with a potential bias.
- **Simile**: It's like a judge weighing the reliability of testimonies in a courtroom.

5. Re-interviewing Witnesses

- **Description**: Re-interviewing witnesses to clarify inconsistencies and gather additional details.
- **Example**: If initial statements are conflicting, the investigator might ask follow-up questions to

understand why the witnesses remember the event differently.

- **Simile**: It's like a teacher asking students to explain their answers to understand their thought process.

6. Consulting Experts

- **Description**: Involving experts, such as accident reconstruction specialists, to provide an objective analysis of the event.
- **Example**: An accident reconstruction expert might use physical evidence and witness statements to recreate the accident and determine what likely happened.
- **Simile**: It's like hiring a specialist to solve a complex puzzle.

7. Analyzing Context and Environment

- **Description**: Considering the context and environment in which the witnesses observed the event.
- **Example**: If one witness was far away and another was close to the accident, their perspectives might differ due to their vantage points.
- **Simile**: It's like understanding that two people watching a play from different seats will have different views of the performance.

Example Scenario: Car Accident Investigation
Imagine a car accident where two witnesses provide conflicting statements:

- **Witness A** says the red car ran a red light and hit the blue car.

- **Witness B** says the blue car was speeding and hit the red car.

Steps Taken by the Investigator:

1. **Detailed Interviews**: The investigator asks both witnesses to describe the accident in detail, noting the time, location, and sequence of events.
2. **Cross-Referencing Statements**: The investigator compares the statements to find common points and discrepancies.
3. **Corroborating with Physical Evidence**: The investigator examines traffic camera footage, skid marks, and vehicle damage to determine the actual events.
4. **Assessing Credibility**: The investigator evaluates the credibility of each witness based on their background and potential biases.
5. **Re-interviewing Witnesses**: The investigator re-interviews the witnesses to clarify inconsistencies and gather more details.
6. **Consulting Experts**: An accident reconstruction expert is consulted to analyze the physical evidence and recreate the accident.
7. **Analyzing Context and Environment**: The investigator considers the witnesses' vantage points and how they might have influenced their perceptions.

By following these steps, investigators can piece together the most accurate version of events, despite conflicting witness statements. This thorough approach ensures a fair and accurate resolution of the claim.

handled fairly and accurately. They must:

- **Navigate Complex Situations**: Investigators often deal with intricate cases that require a deep understanding of various factors, such as legal issues, technical details, and human behavior.

  - **Example**: In a case of suspected arson, an investigator must understand fire patterns, interview witnesses, and analyze financial records to determine the cause.
  - **Simile**: It's like a detective solving a mystery, piecing together clues from different sources.

- **Build Rapport with Claimants**: Establishing trust with claimants is crucial for gathering accurate information and ensuring cooperation.

  - **Example**: An investigator might need to reassure a nervous claimant that their goal is to find the truth and ensure fair treatment.
  - **Simile**: It's like a counselor building trust with a client to help them open up.

- **Make Sound Judgments Under Pressure**: Investigators often work under tight deadlines and must make quick, yet accurate, decisions.

  - **Example**: Deciding whether to approve a claim based on incomplete information requires careful consideration and experience.
  - **Simile**: It's like a surgeon making critical decisions during an operation.

Motivating Factors in Insurance Investigations

To perform optimally, investigators require a conducive work environment and intrinsic motivation.

- **Intrinsic Motivators**: These are internal factors that drive investigators to excel.

  - **Intellectual Challenge**: The complexity of cases keeps investigators engaged and motivated.

    - **Example**: Solving a particularly challenging fraud case can be highly satisfying.
    - **Simile**: It's like a chess player enjoying a tough match.

  - **Sense of Justice**: Many investigators are driven by a desire to ensure fairness and justice.

    - **Example**: Uncovering a fraudulent claim and preventing a scam can be deeply rewarding.
    - **Simile**: It's like a superhero fighting for justice.

  - **Contributing to the Organization's Success**: Knowing that their work helps the company thrive can be a strong motivator.

    - **Example**: Successfully resolving claims efficiently can improve the company's reputation.
    - **Simile**: It's like a team player contributing to a sports team's victory.

- **Extrinsic Motivators**: These are external factors that influence job satisfaction and performance.

- **Career Advancement**: Opportunities for promotion and professional growth.

  - **Example**: An investigator might be motivated by the prospect of becoming a senior investigator or manager.
  - **Simile**: It's like climbing a career ladder.

- **Recognition**: Acknowledgment of their hard work and achievements.

  - **Example**: Receiving an award for outstanding performance can boost morale.
  - **Simile**: It's like a student receiving a gold star for excellent work.

- **Compensation**: Competitive salaries and benefits.

  - **Example**: Knowing that their efforts are financially rewarded can be motivating.
  - **Simile**: It's like receiving a bonus for a job well done.

- **Training and Development**: Opportunities for continuous learning and skill enhancement.

  - **Example**: Attending workshops and courses to stay updated on the latest investigation techniques.
  - **Simile**: It's like a chef learning new recipes to improve their cooking.

- **Work-Life Balance**: Ensuring that work demands do not overwhelm personal life.

  - **Example**: Flexible working hours can help investigators manage stress.
  - **Simile**: It's like balancing on a tightrope, ensuring neither side tips too far.

A supportive organizational culture is essential. Empowerment, feedback, and recognition programs can foster a positive work environment.

Challenges Faced by Insurance Investigators

Investigators operate in a demanding environment with numerous obstacles:

- **Geographical Constraints**: Vast distances, infrastructure challenges, and language barriers can hinder investigations.

  - **Example**: Investigating a claim in a remote village with poor road access.
  - **Simile**: It's like exploring uncharted territory without a map.

- **Legal and Regulatory Hurdles**: Complex legal frameworks and bureaucratic delays can impact efficiency.

  - **Example**: Navigating different state laws and regulations for a multi-state insurance claim.
  - **Simile**: It's like trying to solve a puzzle with constantly changing pieces.

- **Resource Constraints**: Limited manpower, financial resources, and technology can affect investigation quality.

  - **Example**: Handling multiple cases with a small team and limited budget.
  - **Simile**: It's like trying to build a house with only a few tools.

Overcoming these challenges requires resilience, adaptability, and a strong support system within the organization. By addressing these issues effectively, insurance companies can improve the accuracy of claim assessments and protect their financial interests. It's like a well-coordinated team working together to achieve a common goal.

CHAPTER TWENTY-FIVE

Breaking Down the Barriers: Investigator Challenges

Investigators often face various resource constraints that can impact the efficiency and effectiveness of their work. Here are some detailed examples:

Examples of Resource Constraints Faced by Investigators

1. Time Constraints

- **Description**: Limited time to complete investigations due to tight deadlines or urgent cases.
- **Example**: An investigator might have only a few days to gather evidence and submit a report for a high-profile insurance claim.
- **Simile**: It's like trying to finish a marathon in record time while ensuring every step is perfect.

2. Budgetary Constraints

- **Description**: Insufficient financial resources to cover the costs of investigations.
- **Example**: An investigator may need to travel to multiple locations to gather evidence, but the budget only allows for one trip.
- **Simile**: It's like trying to build a house with a limited budget, where every expense must be carefully planned.

3. Manpower Constraints

- **Description**: Limited number of investigators available to handle multiple cases.
- **Example**: A small team of investigators might be overwhelmed with a sudden influx of claims after a natural disaster.
- **Simile**: It's like a small crew trying to manage a large ship during a storm.

4. Technological Constraints

- **Description**: Lack of access to advanced technology and tools needed for thorough investigations.
- **Example**: Investigators might not have access to the latest forensic software or equipment, making it harder to analyze evidence.
- **Simile**: It's like a detective trying to solve a case with outdated tools.

5. Material Constraints

- **Description**: Shortage of physical resources required for investigations.

- **Example**: Limited access to vehicles for on-site inspections or insufficient office supplies for documentation.
- **Simile**: It's like a painter running out of paint in the middle of creating a masterpiece.

6. Geographical Constraints

- **Description**: Challenges related to the location of the investigation sites.
- **Example**: Investigating claims in remote or rural areas where infrastructure is poor and travel is difficult.
- **Simile**: It's like exploring a dense jungle without a clear path.

7. Legal and Regulatory Hurdles

- **Description**: Complex legal frameworks and bureaucratic delays that can slow down investigations.
- **Example**: Navigating different state laws and regulations for a multi-state insurance claim.
- **Simile**: It's like trying to solve a puzzle with constantly changing pieces.

8. Safety Concerns

- **Description**: Risks associated with inspecting accident sites or damaged properties.
- **Example**: Entering a partially collapsed building to assess damage can be dangerous.
- **Simile**: It's like walking through a minefield, where every step must be taken with caution.

9. Availability of Experts

- **Description**: Difficulty in securing the services of qualified experts in a timely manner.
- **Example**: Finding a structural engineer to assess a building collapse might take time.
- **Simile**: It's like searching for a needle in a haystack.

10. Conflicting Expert Opinions

- **Description**: Different experts providing conflicting assessments, making it challenging to reach a definitive conclusion.
- **Example**: One doctor might diagnose a minor injury, while another sees it as severe.
- **Simile**: It's like two chefs arguing over the best recipe for the same dish.

By understanding and addressing these resource constraints, investigators can improve their efficiency and effectiveness, ensuring thorough and accurate investigations. This requires a combination of strategic planning, resource optimization, and support from the organization.

CHAPTER TWENTY-SIX

Maximizing Efficiency: Prioritizing Claims- A Strategic Approach

When investigators face limited resources, prioritizing cases becomes essential to ensure that the most critical and time-sensitive claims are addressed first. Here are some strategies they use, along with examples and similes to illustrate the process:

Strategies for Prioritizing Cases

1. Severity of the Claim

- **Description**: High-severity claims, such as those involving significant financial loss or serious injuries, are prioritized over minor claims.
- **Example**: A claim involving a major fire that destroyed a business will be prioritized over a minor fender-bender.
- **Simile**: It's like a doctor treating a patient with a life-threatening injury before attending to someone with a minor cut.

2. Time Sensitivity

- **Description**: Claims that require immediate attention due to legal deadlines or urgent needs are given priority.
- **Example**: A claim with an impending court date or one where the claimant needs immediate financial assistance for medical treatment.
- **Simile**: It's like a firefighter responding to a house fire before dealing with a small brush fire.

3. Potential for Fraud

- **Description**: Claims that show signs of potential fraud are prioritized to prevent financial losses and maintain the integrity of the insurance process.
- **Example**: A claim with suspicious documentation or a history of similar claims by the same claimant.
- **Simile**: It's like a security guard focusing on a suspicious person in a crowd to prevent theft.

4. Impact on Policyholders

- **Description**: Claims that significantly impact the policyholder's life or business are prioritized to provide timely support.
- **Example**: A claim involving a family's home being uninhabitable due to a natural disaster.
- **Simile**: It's like a teacher helping a struggling student before assisting those who are already doing well.

5. Resource Availability

- **Description**: Prioritizing cases based on the availability of necessary resources, such as experts or specialized equipment.

- **Example**: If a structural engineer is available, a building collapse claim might be prioritized over a simpler vehicle damage claim.
- **Simile**: It's like a chef preparing dishes based on the ingredients they have on hand.

6. Legal and Regulatory Requirements

- **Description**: Ensuring compliance with legal and regulatory deadlines and requirements.
- **Example**: Prioritizing claims that must be resolved within a specific timeframe due to regulatory mandates.
- **Simile**: It's like a student submitting assignments based on their due dates.

Example Scenario: Natural Disaster Claims

Imagine a natural disaster, such as a hurricane, that results in numerous insurance claims. Investigators might prioritize as follows:

1. **High-Severity Claims**: Homes completely destroyed or severely damaged, requiring immediate attention for safety and financial reasons.

   - **Example**: A family's home is uninhabitable, and they need immediate assistance for temporary housing.
   - **Simile**: It's like a rescue team prioritizing people trapped in collapsed buildings.

2. **Time-Sensitive Claims**: Claims with legal deadlines or urgent needs, such as medical treatment for injuries sustained during the disaster.

- Example: A claimant needs urgent medical treatment and financial support.
- Simile: It's like a paramedic treating the most critically injured first.

3. **Potential Fraud Claims**: Claims that show signs of potential fraud, such as exaggerated damage reports or suspicious documentation.

   - Example: A claim with inconsistencies in the damage report compared to the actual condition of the property.
   - Simile: It's like a detective focusing on the most suspicious leads in an investigation.

4. **Impact on Policyholders**: Claims that significantly impact the policyholder's life or business, such as a small business owner whose shop was destroyed.

   - Example: A business owner needs immediate support to rebuild and continue operations.
   - Simile: It's like a community leader helping the most affected families first.

5. **Resource Availability**: Prioritizing based on the availability of experts, such as structural engineers or medical professionals.

   - Example: If a structural engineer is available, they might assess the most severely damaged buildings first.
   - Simile: It's like a chef preparing dishes based on the ingredients they have on hand.

By using these strategies, investigators can effectively manage their limited resources and ensure that the most critical and urgent claims are addressed promptly. This approach helps maintain fairness and efficiency in the claims process.

CHAPTER TWENTY-SEVEN

Motivating Factors in Insurance Investigations: Factors Driving Investigator Performance

Insurance investigations are often characterized by their meticulous nature and the potential for high stakes. These investigations require a unique blend of skills, perseverance, and dedication. To maintain a high level of performance and job satisfaction, investigators need a strong set of motivating factors. These can be broadly categorized into intrinsic and extrinsic motivators, along with the crucial role of organizational culture.

Intrinsic Motivators

1. **Intellectual Challenge:**

- ○ Insurance investigations frequently involve complex puzzles that demand analytical thinking and advanced problem-solving skills. This intellectual stimulation can be highly motivating for individuals who thrive on intellectual challenges and enjoy the process of uncovering hidden truths.

2. **Sense of Justice:**

- ○ Uncovering fraudulent claims and bringing perpetrators to justice can be immensely satisfying. Investigators with a strong sense of justice are driven by the desire to ensure fairness and integrity within the insurance industry. This intrinsic motivation can be a powerful force in maintaining high performance.

3. **Contribution to the Organization:**

- ○ Understanding the significant impact of their investigations on the company's bottom line can be highly motivating for investigators. Knowing that their work directly contributes to the overall success and financial health of the organization can provide a deep sense of purpose and fulfillment.

Extrinsic Motivators

1. **Career Advancement:**

- ○ Opportunities for career growth and promotion are significant motivators. Clear career paths, coupled with performance-based incentives, can encourage investigators to excel in their roles. The prospect of advancing within the organization can drive sustained high performance.

2. **Recognition and Rewards:**

   ◦ Acknowledgment of achievements and performance-based rewards can significantly boost morale and motivation. Recognition from peers and superiors, whether through formal awards or informal praise, reinforces the value of the investigator's contributions.

3. **Competitive Compensation:**

   ◦ A fair and competitive compensation package is essential to attract and retain top talent. Competitive salaries, bonuses, and benefits ensure that investigators feel valued and adequately rewarded for their expertise and hard work.

4. **Training and Development:**

   ◦ Opportunities for continuous learning and skill enhancement are crucial for keeping investigators engaged and motivated. Access to training programs, workshops, and professional development courses helps investigators stay current with industry trends and best practices.

5. **Work-Life Balance:**

- A healthy work-life balance is vital for employee well-being and productivity. Organizations that prioritize flexible working hours, remote work options, and adequate time off can help investigators maintain a balance between their professional and personal lives, reducing burnout and enhancing job satisfaction.

The Role of Organizational Culture

A positive and supportive organizational culture is essential for fostering motivation among investigators. A culture that values teamwork, collaboration, and open communication can create a motivating work environment.

1. **Empowerment:**

    - Allowing investigators to take ownership of their work and make decisions can boost morale and job satisfaction. Empowered employees are more likely to feel invested in their roles and motivated to perform at their best.

2. **Feedback and Coaching:**

    - Regular feedback and coaching are vital for continuous improvement. Constructive feedback helps investigators identify areas for growth, while coaching provides the support and guidance needed to enhance their skills and performance.

3. **Recognition Programs:**

○ Implementing formal recognition programs to celebrate achievements can significantly motivate employees. Recognizing and rewarding outstanding performance fosters a culture of appreciation and encourages others to strive for excellence.

By understanding the factors that motivate insurance investigators, organizations can create a work environment that fosters high performance, job satisfaction, and employee retention. A well-rounded approach that includes both intrinsic and extrinsic motivators, supported by a positive organizational culture, is key to driving investigator performance and achieving organizational success.

CHAPTER TWENTY-EIGHT

The Weight of Responsibility: The Trials and Tribulations of an Insurance Investigator

Insurance investigators face a variety of challenges that can complicate their work and require them to be highly skilled and adaptable. Here are some of the key challenges:

1. Complex Fraud Schemes

Fraudsters often devise intricate schemes to deceive insurance companies. For example, in a staged accident, multiple parties might collude to create a fake car crash. They might use fake witnesses, falsified medical reports, and exaggerated injury claims to defraud the insurance company. Investigators must unravel these layers of deceit to uncover the truth.

2. Regulatory and Legal Constraints

Insurance investigators must comply with various regulations and legal requirements. For instance, in cross-border cases involving international insurance fraud, investigators must navigate different legal systems and regulatory frameworks. This can be particularly challenging when evidence needs to be collected from multiple countries with varying laws on data privacy and evidence handling.

3. Technological Advancements

While technology aids investigations, it also presents challenges. For example, fraudsters might use sophisticated software to alter digital documents or create fake identities. Investigators need to stay updated with the latest forensic tools and techniques to detect such frauds. This includes using advanced data analytics to identify patterns and anomalies in claims data.

4. Data Privacy Concerns

Handling sensitive personal information requires strict adherence to data privacy laws. For example, during an investigation, an investigator might need access to a claimant's medical records. They must ensure that this information is handled securely and in compliance with data protection regulations like GDPR or HIPAA, balancing thorough investigation with privacy concerns.

5. Resource Limitations

Investigative teams often operate with limited resources. For instance, a small team might be tasked with investigating a large number of claims within a short timeframe. This can limit their ability to conduct in-depth investigations and follow up on all leads, potentially allowing some fraudulent claims to slip through the cracks.

6. Ethical Dilemmas

Investigators may face ethical challenges; such as pressure to produce quick results. For example, an investigator might be tempted to cut corners or use questionable methods to meet tight deadlines. Maintaining integrity and ethical standards is crucial, even when faced with such pressures.

7. Reluctant Witnesses

Obtaining cooperation from witnesses can be challenging. For example, in a case of arson for insurance fraud, witnesses might be afraid to come forward due to fear of retaliation from the perpetrators. This reluctance can hinder the collection of crucial evidence needed to prove the fraud.

8. Physical and Emotional Stress

The nature of investigative work can be physically demanding and emotionally taxing. For instance, investigators might have to work long hours, travel frequently, and deal with high-stress situations, such as interviewing hostile witnesses or visiting crime scenes. This can lead to burnout and affect their overall well-being.

9. Evolving Fraud Tactics

Fraud tactics are constantly evolving. For example, with the rise of digital transactions, cyber insurance fraud has become more prevalent. Fraudsters might use phishing attacks to steal personal information and file fraudulent claims. Investigators need to stay updated with the latest trends and techniques in fraud detection and prevention.

10. Interdepartmental Coordination

Effective investigations often require coordination between multiple departments within an organization. For example, an insurance investigator might need to work closely with the legal department, claims adjusters, and IT specialists to gather evidence and build a case. Ensuring smooth communication and collaboration can be challenging, especially in large organizations with complex structures.

By understanding and addressing these challenges, insurance investigators can enhance their effectiveness and contribute to the integrity of the insurance industry.

CHAPTER TWENTY-NINE

A Multi-faceted Skillset: What Makes a Great Insurance Investigator

An effective insurance investigator requires a blend of hard and soft skills to navigate the complexities of the role. These skills can be categorized into technical skills, investigative skills, interpersonal skills, and additional skills.

Technical Skills

1. **Data Analysis:**

   - **Proficiency in using data analytics tools:** Investigators need to be adept at using software like Excel, SQL, or specialized data analysis tools to sift through large volumes of claims data. For example, identifying patterns such as repeated claims from the same individual or anomalies like unusually high claim amounts can help detect potential fraud.

2. **Document Verification:**

   - **Ability to authenticate documents**: Investigators must be skilled in verifying the authenticity of documents such as medical reports, repair invoices, and identification papers. Techniques include checking for signs of forgery, such as inconsistent fonts or altered dates.
   - **Detecting forgeries and inconsistencies**: For instance, an investigator might compare a claimant's signature on different documents to spot discrepancies that indicate forgery.

3. **Legal Knowledge:**

   - **Understanding of insurance contracts, legal procedures, and regulations**: Knowledge of the legal framework governing insurance claims is crucial. For example, understanding the nuances of policy terms can help in determining the legitimacy of a claim and ensuring compliance with legal standards.

4. **Technical Expertise:**

   - **Knowledge of vehicle mechanics, engineering, or other relevant fields**: Specialized claims, such as those involving vehicle accidents, require technical expertise. An investigator might need to understand vehicle damage patterns to assess whether an accident was staged.

5. **IT Proficiency:**

○ **Familiarity with software applications for case management, documentation, and communication:** Proficiency in using case management systems, document management software, and communication tools ensures efficient handling of investigations. For example, using a centralized database to track case progress and store evidence.

Investigative Skills

1. **Problem-solving:**

○ **Ability to analyze complex situations and develop effective investigation strategies:** Investigators must be able to dissect complicated scenarios and devise strategies to uncover the truth. For instance, in a multi-party fraud scheme, they need to identify connections between the involved parties and trace the flow of fraudulent activities.

2. **Critical Thinking:**

○ **Skill in evaluating evidence, identifying inconsistencies, and drawing logical conclusions:** Critical thinking is essential for assessing the validity of evidence. For example, an investigator might notice that the timeline of events provided by a claimant doesn't match the evidence, indicating possible fraud.

3. **Attention to Detail:**

- **Meticulousness in examining documents, inspecting scenes, and gathering information**: Attention to detail is crucial for spotting subtle clues. For instance, noticing a minor discrepancy in a medical report that suggests it has been altered.

4. **Interviewing Skills**:

- **Ability to conduct effective interviews with claimants, witnesses, and other parties involved**: Skilled interviewing techniques help in extracting accurate information. For example, using open-ended questions to encourage detailed responses and observing body language for signs of deception.

5. **Report Writing**:

- **Clear and concise communication of investigation findings through written reports**: Effective report writing is essential for documenting findings and presenting them to stakeholders. A well-written report should clearly outline the evidence, analysis, and conclusions.

Interpersonal Skills

1. **Communication**:

- **Effective verbal and written communication skills to interact with various stakeholders**: Strong communication skills are necessary for explaining complex findings to non-experts, such as insurance adjusters or legal teams.

2. **Negotiation:**

    ◦ **Ability to negotiate with claimants, repair shops, and other parties**: Negotiation skills are important for resolving disputes and reaching settlements. For example, negotiating with a repair shop to verify the authenticity of an invoice.

3. **Interpersonal Skills:**

    ◦ **Building rapport and trust with claimants and witnesses**: Establishing trust is key to obtaining cooperation and accurate information. For instance, showing empathy and understanding can encourage a reluctant witness to share crucial details.

4. **Ethical Conduct:**

    ◦ **Adherence to professional ethics and maintaining confidentiality**: Investigators must uphold high ethical standards and ensure confidentiality. This includes handling sensitive information with discretion and avoiding conflicts of interest.

Additional Skills

1. **Time Management:**

    ◦ **Ability to prioritize tasks and manage multiple cases simultaneously**: Effective time management ensures that investigations are conducted efficiently. For example, using project management tools to track deadlines and allocate resources.

2. **Adaptability:**

    - **Flexibility to handle diverse cases and changing circumstances**: Investigators must be adaptable to different types of cases and evolving situations. For instance, quickly adjusting investigation strategies in response to new evidence.

3. **Resilience:**

    - **Ability to cope with stress and maintain focus under pressure**: Resilience is crucial for handling the demands of investigative work. This includes managing high-stress situations, such as dealing with hostile witnesses or working long hours to meet deadlines.

Possessing a combination of these skills enables investigators to conduct thorough, efficient, and effective investigations, ultimately protecting the insurer's interests.

CHAPTER THIRTY

Surveillance in Insurance Investigations: The Role of Surveillance in Investigations

Surveillance is a critical tactical tool employed by insurance investigators to gather evidence of suspicious activity or verify the legitimacy of claims. It plays a pivotal role in uncovering fraudulent activities and ensuring the integrity of the insurance process. However, it is essential to conduct surveillance discreetly and ethically, adhering to legal and privacy regulations to protect the rights of individuals involved.

Types of Surveillance

1. **Physical Surveillance:**

- ◦ **In-person Observation**: This involves directly observing individuals or locations. Techniques include stakeouts, where investigators maintain a fixed observation point to monitor a person, place, or vehicle. For example, an investigator might conduct a stakeout outside a claimant's residence to verify their reported injuries.
- ◦ **Following Subjects**: Investigators may follow subjects by vehicle or on foot to track their movements and activities. This can help gather evidence of inconsistencies in their claims, such as a supposedly injured person engaging in physical activities.
- ◦ **Site Visits**: Conducting visits to specific locations, such as accident sites or places of employment, to gather information and verify details provided in claims.

2. **Electronic Surveillance:**

- ◦ **Video Surveillance**: Utilizing cameras to record activities and movements. This can include installing hidden cameras in strategic locations to capture evidence of fraudulent behavior.
- ◦ **GPS Tracking**: Employing GPS devices to monitor the location of vehicles or individuals. For instance, tracking a vehicle to verify its use and location during the time of a reported theft.
- ◦ **Phone Tapping (with Legal Authorization)**: In some cases, investigators may use phone tapping to monitor communications, provided they have obtained the necessary legal authorization.

3. **Social Media Surveillance:**

   - **Monitoring Online Activities:** Investigators can gather valuable information by monitoring an individual's social media profiles. This can reveal details about their lifestyle, associates, and potential inconsistencies in their claims. For example, a claimant who reports being unable to work due to injury might post photos of themselves engaging in physical activities on social media.

Surveillance Techniques

1. **Stakeouts:**

   - **Fixed Observation Points:** Maintaining a fixed position to monitor a person, place, or vehicle. This technique is often used to observe the daily routines and activities of a subject without their knowledge.

2. **Follows:**

   - **Tracking Movements:** Following a subject by vehicle or on foot to observe their activities and interactions. This can help gather evidence of inconsistencies in their claims, such as a claimant visiting multiple doctors to obtain prescriptions fraudulently.

3. **Undercover Operations:**

   - **Assuming False Identities:** Investigators may assume false identities to infiltrate groups or organizations involved in fraudulent activities. For example, an investigator might pose as a potential customer to gather information about a fraudulent insurance scheme.

4. **Video Surveillance**:

   ◦ **Recording Activities**: Using cameras to capture evidence of fraudulent behavior. This can include installing hidden cameras in locations where fraudulent activities are suspected to occur.

5. **GPS Tracking**:

   ◦ **Monitoring Locations**: Employing GPS devices to track the movements of vehicles or individuals. This can help verify the accuracy of claims, such as tracking a vehicle reported as stolen to its actual location.

Legal and Ethical Considerations

1. **Privacy Laws**:

   ◦ **Adherence to Data Protection Laws**: Investigators must comply with data protection and privacy laws to ensure that surveillance activities do not infringe on individuals' rights. This includes obtaining necessary permissions and ensuring that collected data is securely stored and handled.

2. **Consent**:

- **Obtaining Necessary Permissions**: In certain cases, obtaining consent for surveillance might be necessary. For example, using GPS tracking devices may require the consent of the vehicle owner.

3. **Ethical Guidelines:**

- **Conducting Surveillance Ethically**: Ensuring that surveillance is conducted ethically and without infringing on the rights of individuals. This includes avoiding intrusive or deceptive practices that could harm the subjects of surveillance.

4. **Evidence Admissibility:**

- **Legal Compliance for Court Admissibility**: Gathering evidence in a legally compliant manner is essential for its admissibility in court. This includes ensuring that surveillance activities are conducted within the bounds of the law and that collected evidence is properly documented and preserved.

Challenges and Limitations

1. **Resource Intensive:**

- **Manpower and Financial Resources**: Surveillance operations require significant manpower and financial resources. This includes the cost of equipment, personnel, and time spent on surveillance activities.

2. **Counter-Surveillance:**

- ○ **Detection by Fraudsters**: Fraudsters may employ counter-surveillance measures to detect and evade surveillance activities. This can include using their own surveillance techniques to monitor investigators or employing tactics to mislead investigators.

3. **Technological Limitations:**

- ○ **Advances and Hindrances**: Advances in technology can both enhance and hinder surveillance capabilities. For example, while GPS tracking devices can provide precise location data, they can also be detected and disabled by savvy fraudsters.

4. **Ethical Dilemmas:**

- ○ **Balancing Evidence and Privacy**: Balancing the need for evidence with the protection of privacy can present ethical challenges. Investigators must navigate these dilemmas carefully to ensure that their actions are both effective and ethical.

Surveillance, when conducted properly, is a powerful tool in the arsenal of insurance investigators. By understanding and addressing the legal, ethical, and practical challenges, investigators can effectively use surveillance to uncover fraud and protect the interests of insurers.

CHAPTER THIRTY-ONE

Undercover Investigations in Insurance: The Use of Undercover Operations in Complex Cases

Undercover investigations are a specialized and highly effective tool employed in complex insurance fraud cases. These operations involve deploying investigators to infiltrate fraudulent networks or assume false identities to gather critical evidence. The success of such investigations hinges on meticulous planning, skilled personnel, and strict adherence to legal and ethical guidelines.

Key Applications

1. **Organized Fraud Rings:**

   ◦ **Exposing Networks:** Undercover operations are instrumental in uncovering organized fraud rings involved in activities such as staged accidents, inflated claims, and other fraudulent schemes. For example, an investigator might pose as a participant in a staged accident ring to gather evidence on how the fraud is orchestrated and identify key players involved.

2. **Claim Exaggeration:**

   ◦ **Verifying Injuries or Damages**: Investigators may assume the role of a potential customer or employee at a repair shop to verify the extent of injuries or damages claimed. For instance, an investigator might pose as a customer seeking repairs to observe if a repair shop is inflating damage estimates or colluding with claimants to exaggerate claims.

3. **Policy Fraud:**

   ◦ **Uncovering False Claims**: Undercover operations can help uncover instances of policy fraud, such as false claims or misrepresentations. An investigator might pose as an insurance agent to interact with individuals suspected of providing false information on their insurance applications or claims.

Challenges and Considerations

1. **Legal and Ethical Implications:**

   ◦ **Adherence to Guidelines**: Undercover investigations must adhere to strict legal and ethical guidelines to ensure the admissibility of evidence. Investigators must be well-versed in the legal boundaries of their operations to avoid actions that could compromise the investigation or lead to legal repercussions.

2. **Risk to Investigators:**

   - **Safety and Well-being**: Undercover operations can pose significant risks to the investigator's safety and well-being. Investigators may find themselves in potentially dangerous situations, requiring them to have strong situational awareness and contingency plans to ensure their safety.

3. **Operational Complexity:**

   - **Meticulous Planning and Coordination**: Planning and executing undercover investigations require meticulous planning and coordination. This includes developing a cover story, establishing a credible identity, and coordinating with other team members to ensure seamless execution.

4. **Evidence Preservation:**

   - **Integrity and Admissibility**: Ensuring the integrity and admissibility of evidence collected through undercover operations is crucial. Investigators must follow proper procedures for documenting and preserving evidence to ensure it can be used effectively in legal proceedings.

Success Factors

1. **Thorough Planning**:

   ◦ **Preparation and Risk Assessment**: Careful preparation and risk assessment are essential for the success of undercover operations. This includes conducting background research, developing a detailed plan, and identifying potential risks and mitigation strategies.

2. **Skilled Personnel**:

   ◦ **Acting Skills, Intelligence, and Adaptability**: Investigators must possess strong acting skills, intelligence, and adaptability to convincingly assume false identities and navigate complex situations. They must be able to think on their feet and adjust their approach as needed.

3. **Collaboration**:

   ◦ **Coordination with Investigative Teams and Law Enforcement**: Effective coordination with other investigative teams and law enforcement is crucial. Collaboration ensures that all aspects of the investigation are covered and that evidence is collected and handled properly.

4. **Documentation**:

   ◦ **Detailed Records of Activities**: Maintaining detailed records of undercover activities is vital for legal purposes. This includes documenting interactions, observations, and evidence collected during the operation to provide a clear and comprehensive account of the investigation.

Undercover investigations are a powerful tool in the fight against insurance fraud. When used judiciously and with careful consideration of the potential risks and rewards, they can provide invaluable insights and evidence to protect the interests of insurers and uphold the integrity of the insurance industry.

The Paradox of Professionalism in Indian Insurance Investigations

The Indian insurance industry finds itself in a curious predicament, much like a ship with a skilled captain but no navigational charts. On one hand, there's a growing recognition of the need for professional, skilled investigators to combat the rising tide of insurance fraud. On the other, the industry lacks a standardized framework for selecting and empaneling investigators. This, coupled with the often inadequate skillset of insurance investigation department managers, creates a complex and challenging environment.

The Need for Professionalism

The insurance industry is increasingly grappling with sophisticated fraud schemes, akin to a chess game where fraudsters are always thinking several moves ahead. These schemes require investigators with specialized skills in areas such as forensic accounting, digital forensics, and legal acumen. A professional investigator can:

- **Enhance Claim Accuracy**: By meticulously examining claims, they can prevent overpayments and underpayments. For example, an investigator with forensic accounting skills can detect discrepancies in financial records that might indicate fraud.
- **Deter Fraud**: The presence of skilled investigators can act as a deterrent to potential fraudsters, much like a security camera deters shoplifters.
- **Protect the Insurer's Reputation**: Successful investigations can safeguard the insurer's image by demonstrating a commitment to fairness and transparency. For instance, uncovering a major fraud scheme and bringing the perpetrators to justice can enhance public trust in the insurer.

Lack of Standardized Empanelment Process

The absence of a standardized process for empaneling investigators has led to several issues, similar to a sports team without a clear selection criteria for its players:

- **Inconsistency in Selection Criteria**: Different insurers employ varying criteria, making it difficult for investigators to meet the requirements of multiple companies. This is like a player trying to adapt to different rules in every game.
- **Subjectivity in the Selection Process**: The selection often relies on personal relationships or recommendations rather than objective evaluations of qualifications. This can be compared to hiring a player based on friendship rather than skill.

- **Potential for Favoritism**: This lack of standardization can create opportunities for favoritism and corruption, much like a biased referee favoring one team over another.
- **Limited Access to Quality Investigators**: Without a clear pathway to empanelment, many skilled investigators might be discouraged from entering the field, akin to talented players being sidelined due to unclear selection processes.

The Challenge of Inadequate Managerial Skillset

The effectiveness of an investigation team is heavily influenced by the leadership provided by the investigation department manager. Unfortunately, many managers lack the necessary skills to oversee complex investigations. This manifests in several ways:

- **Limited Understanding of Investigative Techniques**: Managers without investigative experience may struggle to provide guidance to their team, similar to a coach who has never played the sport.
- **Inability to Assess Investigator Performance**: A lack of understanding of investigative standards can hinder the evaluation of staff, much like a coach unable to recognize a player's strengths and weaknesses.
- **Difficulty in Managing Relationships with External Stakeholders**: Effective collaboration with law enforcement, legal departments, and external investigators requires strong interpersonal and negotiation skills. This is akin to a coach who cannot effectively communicate with referees and other teams.
- **Strategic Oversight**: Without a clear strategic vision, the investigation department may operate in silos,

leading to inefficiencies, much like a team playing without a game plan.

The Way Forward

To address these challenges, the insurance industry must take the following steps:

- **Develop a Standardized Empanelment Process**: This should include clear eligibility criteria, a rigorous evaluation process, and ongoing performance assessments. Think of it as creating a unified rulebook for selecting the best players.
- **Invest in Training and Development**: Insurance companies should invest in training programs for investigation department managers to enhance their skills and knowledge. This is similar to providing coaches with advanced training to improve their coaching techniques.
- **Establish Industry Associations**: Creating platforms for knowledge sharing and best practice exchange can improve the overall quality of investigations. This is like forming a league where teams can share strategies and improve collectively.
- **Foster Collaboration with Law Enforcement**: Stronger partnerships with law enforcement can help in combating complex fraud schemes. This is akin to teams working together with referees to ensure fair play.
- **Embrace Technology**: Utilizing advanced technologies can enhance investigative capabilities and improve efficiency. This is like equipping players with the best gear to enhance their performance.

By implementing these measures, the Indian insurance industry can strengthen its investigative capabilities and better protect its interests, much like a well-coached team with a clear strategy and skilled players can dominate the game.

CHAPTER THIRTY-THREE

The Complexities of Third-Party Insurance Investigations: A Case for Scientific Fee Structure

Third-party insurance investigations are a cornerstone of the insurance industry, much like the foundation of a building. However, the fee structures governing these investigations often fall short of accurately reflecting the complexities and challenges involved. This disparity between the demanding nature of the work and the often standardized fee models creates a systemic imbalance that compromises the quality of investigations.

The Nature of the Beast: Challenges in Third-Party Investigations

Third-party investigations demand a multifaceted skill set, akin to a detective who must be part lawyer, part doctor, and part engineer. Investigators must not only possess a keen eye for detail but also a deep understanding of legal, medical, and technical aspects. The geographical expanse of India, particularly the stark contrast between urban and rural areas, exacerbates these challenges.

1. **Geographical Disparities:**

    ○ **Vast Distances**: The vast distances between accident sites, hospitals, police stations, and other relevant locations in rural India significantly increase the time, effort, and financial resources required for investigations. For instance, an investigator in Karnataka might need to travel hundreds of kilometers to gather evidence, often in regions with limited infrastructure. This is like a marathon runner having to navigate through rough terrain, making the journey much more arduous.

2. **Document Procurement Challenges:**

    ○ **Bureaucratic Ordeals**: Obtaining essential documents such as police reports, medical records, and witness statements can be a bureaucratic ordeal, involving multiple agencies and time-consuming procedures. Corruption is not uncommon, further complicating the process. Imagine trying to retrieve a needle from a haystack, where each piece of hay represents a different bureaucratic hurdle.

3. **Complex Human Interactions:**

    ○ **Diverse Cultural and Socioeconomic Backgrounds**: Dealing with claimants, witnesses, and insurance personnel requires strong interpersonal skills and the ability to navigate diverse cultural and socioeconomic backgrounds. This is similar to a diplomat who must understand and respect various cultural nuances to build trust and gather information effectively.

4. **Time Constraints:**

   - **Tight Deadlines:** The insurance industry operates on tight deadlines, pressuring investigators to deliver results efficiently. This can lead to rushed investigations and compromised quality. It's like a chef being asked to prepare a gourmet meal in a fast-food timeframe, where the quality of the dish inevitably suffers.

The Inadequacy of Standardized Fee Structures

The current fee structure for third-party investigations often fails to account for the varying levels of complexity and effort required for different cases. A one-size-fits-all approach overlooks the significant disparities between urban and rural investigations.

1. **Disregard for Geographical Factors:**

   - **Geographical Challenges:** Fee structures rarely consider the geographical challenges faced by investigators, particularly those working in remote areas. This is akin to paying a delivery driver the same rate regardless of whether they are delivering across town or across the country.

2. **Underestimation of Time and Effort:**

    ◦ **Complexity of Cases**: The complexity of many cases demands substantial time and effort, which is often not adequately compensated. Imagine a sculptor being paid the same for a simple carving as for an intricate masterpiece; the effort and skill required are vastly different.

3. **Lack of Incentive for Quality:**

    ◦ **Quality of Investigations**: Without a fee structure that rewards thorough and accurate investigations, there is a risk of investigators cutting corners to meet deadlines. This is like a student rushing through an exam to finish on time, potentially missing important details and making errors.

4. **Erosion of Professional Standards:**

    ◦ **Tight Budgets**: The pressure to work within tight budgets can lead to a decline in the quality of investigations, as investigators may be forced to compromise on resources and expertise. It's like a construction company using substandard materials to stay within budget, resulting in a weaker structure.

Towards a Scientific Fee Structure

To address these issues, a scientific and data-driven approach to fee determination is essential. This should involve:

1. **Detailed Case Categorization:**

- **Classification System**: Developing a classification system for cases based on factors such as geographical location, complexity, and the extent of investigation required. This is similar to categorizing medical procedures based on their complexity and required resources.

2. **Time and Effort Assessment:**

- **Accurate Measurement**: Accurately measuring the time spent on various investigative activities, including travel, document collection, witness interviews, and report writing. Think of it as a meticulous accountant tracking every expense to ensure accurate billing.

3. **Cost Analysis:**

- **Identifying Costs**: Identifying the direct and indirect costs associated with investigations, such as travel expenses, personnel costs, and overhead. This is like a business calculating the true cost of producing a product, including raw materials, labor, and overhead.

4. **Risk Assessment:**

- **Incorporating Risk Factors**: Incorporating factors such as the likelihood of fraud, the potential value of the claim, and the complexity of the legal environment. This is akin to an insurance company assessing the risk factors before issuing a policy.

By implementing a fee structure that reflects the true costs and complexities of investigations, the insurance industry can ensure fair compensation for investigators, maintain high standards of professionalism, and ultimately protect its interests. This approach is like building a house on a solid foundation, ensuring stability and durability for the long term.

Beyond the Boundaries: Collaborative Strategies for Insurance Investigations

Improving efficiency in insurance investigations requires a collaborative approach between insurance companies and investigators. Here are several strategies to enhance this collaboration, along with examples and analogies to illustrate each point:

1. Clear Communication Channels

- **Establishing Open Lines of Communication**: Insurance companies should set up clear and direct communication channels with investigators. This ensures that both parties are on the same page regarding case details, expectations, and timelines. Think of it as a well-coordinated relay race where the baton (information) is smoothly passed between runners (investigators and insurers).

2. Regular Training and Workshops

- **Joint Training Sessions**: Organizing regular training sessions and workshops can help both investigators and insurance company staff stay updated on the latest fraud detection techniques, legal requirements, and industry best practices. This is similar to a sports team regularly practicing together to improve their coordination and performance.

3. Access to Resources and Tools

- **Providing Necessary Tools**: Insurance companies should ensure that investigators have access to the necessary resources and tools, such as advanced data analytics software, forensic tools, and secure communication platforms. This is like equipping a carpenter with high-quality tools to ensure they can work efficiently and effectively.

4. Standardized Procedures

- **Developing Standard Operating Procedures (SOPs)**: Creating standardized procedures for investigations can help streamline processes and ensure consistency. For example, having a clear protocol for evidence collection and documentation can reduce errors and improve the quality of investigations. This is akin to a recipe that ensures every chef in a restaurant prepares the dish the same way, maintaining quality and consistency.

5. Performance Metrics and Feedback

- **Implementing Performance Metrics**: Establishing clear performance metrics and regularly reviewing them can help identify areas for improvement. Providing constructive feedback to investigators based on these metrics can enhance their performance. This is similar to a coach reviewing game footage with players to highlight strengths and areas for improvement.

6. Collaborative Case Management Systems

- **Using Integrated Case Management Systems**: Implementing integrated case management systems that allow real-time updates and information sharing can improve coordination between insurance companies and investigators. This is like a project management tool that keeps all team members informed and aligned on project progress.

7. Incentive Programs

- **Rewarding High Performance**: Developing incentive programs to reward investigators for thorough and efficient investigations can motivate them to maintain high standards. This is similar to employee recognition programs that reward outstanding performance and encourage others to strive for excellence.

8. Regular Meetings and Updates

- **Scheduled Check-ins**: Holding regular meetings to discuss ongoing cases, share updates, and address any challenges can foster a collaborative environment. This is like a weekly team meeting where everyone shares their progress and plans for the upcoming week.

9. Legal and Ethical Compliance

- **Ensuring Compliance**: Both parties should work together to ensure that all investigations comply with legal and ethical standards. This includes adhering to data privacy laws and maintaining the integrity of the investigation process. Think of it as a referee ensuring that all players follow the rules of the game to maintain fairness.

10. Feedback Loop

- **Creating a Feedback Loop**: Establishing a feedback loop where investigators can provide insights and suggestions to insurance companies can help improve processes and policies. This is similar to a suggestion box in a workplace where employees can share ideas for improvement.

Insurance investigators face several challenges when collaborating with insurance companies. These challenges can hinder the efficiency and effectiveness of investigations. Here are some key challenges, along with examples and analogies to illustrate them:

1. Communication Barriers

- **Lack of Clear Communication**: Miscommunication or lack of clear communication channels can lead to misunderstandings and delays. For example, if an investigator is not promptly informed about new evidence or changes in the case, it can result in missed opportunities to gather crucial information. This is akin to a relay race where the baton is dropped due to poor coordination between runners.

2. Resource Constraints

- **Limited Access to Resources**: Investigators often face limitations in accessing necessary resources such as advanced forensic tools, data analytics software, and secure communication platforms. This can impede their ability to conduct thorough investigations. Imagine a detective trying to solve a complex case without access to a crime lab or modern investigative tools.

3. Inconsistent Procedures

- **Lack of Standardized Procedures**: Different insurance companies may have varying procedures and protocols for investigations. This inconsistency can create confusion and inefficiencies. It's like a chef having to adapt to different kitchen setups and recipes every time they cook, leading to potential mistakes and delays.

4. Time Pressure

- **Tight Deadlines**: The insurance industry often operates under tight deadlines, pressuring investigators to deliver results quickly. This can lead to rushed investigations and compromised quality. It's similar to a student cramming for an exam at the last minute, where the quality of learning is compromised due to time constraints.

5. Legal and Ethical Challenges

- **Navigating Legal and Ethical Boundaries**: Investigators must ensure that their methods comply with legal and ethical standards. This can be challenging, especially when dealing with sensitive information or complex legal environments. Think of it as walking a tightrope, where one misstep can lead to serious consequences.

6. Data Privacy Concerns

- **Handling Sensitive Information**: Investigators often deal with sensitive personal information, requiring strict adherence to data privacy laws. Ensuring data security while sharing information with insurance companies can be challenging. This is like a bank ensuring the security of its vaults while allowing access to authorized personnel.

7. Interdepartmental Coordination

- **Coordination with Multiple Departments**: Effective investigations often require collaboration with various departments within the insurance company, such as legal, claims, and IT. Ensuring smooth coordination can be difficult, especially in large organizations. It's like an orchestra where each section must play in harmony to create a cohesive performance.

8. Resistance from Stakeholders

- **Uncooperative Claimants and Witnesses**: Investigators may encounter resistance from claimants, witnesses, or even internal staff, making it difficult to gather accurate information. This is akin to a journalist trying to get a story from reluctant sources who are unwilling to share information.

9. Performance Metrics and Evaluation

- **Lack of Clear Performance Metrics**: Without clear performance metrics, it can be challenging to evaluate the effectiveness of investigators and identify areas for improvement. This is like a sports team playing without a scoreboard, where players are unsure of their performance and progress.

10. Cultural and Socioeconomic Differences

- **Navigating Diverse Backgrounds**: Investigators often deal with individuals from diverse cultural and socioeconomic backgrounds, requiring strong interpersonal skills and cultural sensitivity. This is similar to a diplomat who must navigate different cultural norms and practices to build trust and gather information effectively.

By understanding and addressing these challenges, insurance companies and investigators can work together more effectively, improving the efficiency and quality of insurance investigations. This collaborative approach ensures that both parties are aligned in their goals and can leverage each other's strengths to combat insurance fraud more effectively.

By implementing these strategies, insurance companies and investigators can work together more effectively, improving the efficiency and quality of insurance investigations. This collaborative approach ensures that both parties are aligned in their goals and can leverage each other's strengths to combat insurance fraud more effectively.

References & Terms

References:

Insurance Fraud - Tookitaki www.tookitaki.com

What is insurance fraud and what are its consequences? - Superscript gosuperscript.com,

Types of Car Insurance Fraud | Bankrate www.bankrate.com

Battle Against Insurance Frauds in India - IDfy www.idfy.com

Revealed – the 10 worst insurance fraud cases of all time www.insurancebusinessmag.com

Medical Billing Fraud - Constantine Cannon constantinecannon.com

Why is it important to enhance fraud management for insurance industry? - Subex www.subex.com

Background on: Insurance fraud | III - Insurance Information Institut www.iii.org

What is Auto Insurance Fraud? - State of Michigan www.michigan.gov

What Is Car Insurance Fraud? | Progressive www.progressive.com

Types of Car Insurance Fraud | Bankrate www.bankrate.com

Car Insurance Fraud In India & How To Avoid It? - Policybazaar www.policybazaar.com

How Exaggerating Your Injury Claim Can Backfire • Carter & Carter www.candcsolicitors.co.uk

Deterring Employee Internal Fraud in Insurance Companies - Insightful www.insightful.io

Digital Challenges Facing the Insurance Industry (2024) - Whatfix whatfix.com

General Terms

- **Claim:** A formal request for compensation from an insurance company due to a loss.
- **Policyholder:** An individual or entity insured under an insurance policy.
- **Insurer:** An insurance company that provides coverage.
- **Fraud:** Intentional deception or misrepresentation to gain financial advantage.

Investigation Terms

- **Investigator:** A person employed by an insurance company to investigate claims.
- **Verification:** The process of confirming the accuracy and legitimacy of a claim.
- **Loss Assessment:** Determining the financial value of a loss.
- **Subrogation:** The right of an insurer to pursue recovery from a third party responsible for a loss.
- **Salvage:** The recoverable value of damaged property.
- **Depreciation:** The decrease in value of an asset over time.
- **Underwriting:** The process of assessing risk and determining insurance coverage.

Legal and Financial Terms

- **Fraudulent Conversion:** The unlawful appropriation of property or money entrusted to one's care.
- **Embezzlement:** The theft of funds or property by a person entrusted with its care.
- **Larceny:** The unlawful taking of another person's

property.
- **Forensic Accounting:** The application of accounting, auditing, and investigative skills to examine financial data.

Other Terms

- **Claimants:** Individuals or entities filing a claim.
- **Policyholder:** The individual or entity covered by an insurance policy.
- **Insured:** The person or property covered by an insurance policy.
- **Insurer:** The insurance company providing coverage.